Bibliographic information published by the German National Library:

The German National Library lists this publication in the National Bibliography; detailed bibliographic data are available on the Internet at http://dnb.dnb.de .

Imprint:

Copyright © 2018 GRIN Verlag
Print and binding: Books on Demand GmbH, Norderstedt Germany
ISBN: 9783668765016

This book at GRIN:

https://www.grin.com/document/432230

Artur Sahakjan

A Review of Recent Advancements in Deep Reinforcement Learning

GRIN Verlag

GRIN - Your knowledge has value

Since its foundation in 1998, GRIN has specialized in publishing academic texts by students, college teachers and other academics as e-book and printed book. The website www.grin.com is an ideal platform for presenting term papers, final papers, scientific essays, dissertations and specialist books.

UNIVERSITY OF DUISBURG-ESSEN

BACHELOR THESIS

A Review of Recent Advancements in Deep Reinforcement Learning

---

SUBMITTED TO THE FACULTY OF BUSINESS ADMINISTRATION AND
ECONOMICS

Author:

Artur Sahakjan

Winter Term 2017/18

March 28, 2018

Abstract

Reinforcement learning is a learning problem in which an actor has to behave optimally in its environment (Kaelbling et al., 1996, p. 237). Deep learning methods, on the other hand, are a subclass of representation learning, which in turn focuses on extracting the necessary features for the task (e.g. classification or detection) (Lecun et al., 2015, p. 436). As such, they serve as powerful function approximators. The combination of those two paradigm results in deep reinforcement learning. This thesis gives an overview of the recent advancement in the field. The results are divided into two broad research directions: value-based and policy-based approaches.

This research shows several algorithms from those directions and how they perform. Finally, multiple open research questions are addressed and new research directions are proposed.

Zusammenfassung

"Reinforcement learning" ist ein Lernproblem, in dem ein Agent das Ziel hat, sich optimal in seiner Umgebung zu verhalten (Kaelbling et al., 1996, p. 237). "Deep learning" Methoden hingegen sind in der Lage, eine Funktion zu erlernen, die möglichst präzise das Verhältnis von Input zu Output ihrer Trainingsdaten symbolisiert (Lecun et al., 2015, p. 436). Die Kombination dieser zwei Paradigmen resultiert in "deep reinforcement learning". Das Ziel dieser Arbeit ist es, eine Übersicht über "deep reinforcement learning" zu geben, welche grob in zwei Forschungsrichtungen geteilt werden kann: wertorientierte- und verhaltensorientierte Ansätze.

Diese Arbeit führt mehrere Algorithmen dieser Bereiche auf und vergleicht deren Leistung. Zum Schluss werden noch offene Fragen angezeigt und weitere Forschungsrichtungen ermittelt.

List of Abbreviations

A3C   Asynchronous Advantage Actor-Critic

AI   Artificial Intelligence

BC   Behavior Characteristic

CRN   Common Random Numbers

CNN   Convolutional Neural Network

D-DPG   Deep Deterministic Policy Gradient

DL   Deep Learning

DRL   Deep Reinforcement Learning

DQN   Deep Q-Network

DPG   Deterministic Policy Gradient

DP   Dynamic Programming

ES   Evolution Strategies

FNN   Feedforward Neural Network

GA   Genetic Algorithm

GPU   Graphical Processing Unit

IS   Importance-Sampling

IQL   Independent Q-Learning

IRL   Inverse Reinforcement Learning

KL   Kullback-Leibler

MARL   Multi-Agent Reinforcement Learning

ML	Machine Learning
MLP	Multilayer Perceptron
MC	Monte Carlo
MCTS	Monte Carlo Tree Search
MDP	Markov Decision Process
MOBA	Multiplayer Online Battle Arena
NES	Natural Evolution Strategies
RL	Reinforcement Learning
SGD	Stochastic Gradient Descent
TD	Temporal Difference
TRPO	Trust Region Policy Optimization

List of Figures

List of Tables

List of Algorithms

Table of Contents

1 Introduction

Reinforcement learning (RL) is defined as a class of problem in which an agent has to behave optimally in its environment (Kaelbling et al., 1996, p. 237). For every action the agent takes it receives a reward that indicates to the agent how useful that action was. The action taken by the agent directly influences the future states the agent will end up in. Hence, the goal of the agent is to pick a series of actions that will result in the highest possible reward (Sutton and Barto, 2017, p. 1-5).

One of the key differences between RL as opposed to supervised learning is the lack of a teacher (Kaelbling et al., 1996, p. 239). Whereas in supervised learning the learner is immediately told the error between the predicted and actual output, in RL the agent has no knowledge whether the taken action was, in fact, optimal.

For tasks in which the agent deals with a great state and action space, some form of generalization is needed (Sutton and Barto, 2017, p. 158). An example here would be the case of a self-driving car. It has many types of input, ranging from images from its many cameras and other sensory data like velocity of the car or the outside temperature. At every time-step the car would *see* its environment slightly different than before. At one point there may be a red car driving next to it and later there could be a car with the same model but with a different color. From the point of view of the agent, these would be entirely different states even though the agent should behave the same in both cases. In other words, to prevent the agent from dealing with overwhelmingly many states, it should generalize from experience.

In the last few years, deep learning (Lecun et al., 2015) has shown great success in terms of generalization and has since been used extensively in modern RL methods. Deep learning (DL) delivers very powerful function approximations that have shown stunning performance in different domains, such as mastering the ancient Chinese board game Go (Silver et al., 2017) or playing the multiplayer online battle arena (MOBA) game of Dota 2 (OpenAI, n.d.)

Combining these two paradigms results in deep reinforcement learning (DRL). Here, RL defines the objective, i.e. what the agent wants to achieve while DL on the other hand provides the mechanism to reach the agent's goal (Silver, 2016, slide 5).

Across a wide variety of domains in machine learning (ML) there has been an ever increasing pace of research over the last recent years. New algorithms emerge between shortening time intervals while new research questions are revealed. To not lose sight of the greater picture and to keep track with the accelerating research, the need for an all encompassing view increases.

As such, the goal of this thesis is twofold: first, this thesis will provide a clear overview of the most recent achievements in the field of DRL, focusing primarily on the algorithms; and secondly, it will emphasize new research directions for the future.

The remainder of this thesis is organized as follows. The next chapter will cover how the research for this thesis was conducted, where the sources for the literature and the way they were reviewed will be shown. On the same note, several other closely related papers that influenced this thesis will be mentioned. Chapter three will lay the foundations for this thesis. Before one can understand the algorithms and methods of recent studies, it is vital to know what those were built upon. Here, the fundamental aspects of RL and DL will be covered. The fourth chapter shows the results. This chapter will discuss the recent achievements and their algorithms and techniques. This structure of this chapter is, in parts, derived from the talk at ICML held by David Silver in 2016 (see section 2.1). Chapter five will focus on existing problems and research gaps. The last chapter, six, will summarize this thesis and give a conclusion.

2 Research Method

The first section of this chapter will be dedicated to the related work. Afterwards, the way this research was conducted will be laid out. The sources, and the literature itself, will be described.

2.1 Related Work

Giving overviews in research field is usually common practice and occurs periodically. RL is no exception and as such, there have already been several overviews. One of the earliest overviews were given by Kaelbling et al. (1996). Their survey focused on dynamic programming and model-free methods, such as Q-Learning and TD-Learning. A more formal view on the matter was given by Gosavi (2009), "aimed at *uncovering the mathematical roots* of this science [...]" (Gosavi, 2009).

Kober et al. (2012) gave a survey, where the authors focused on RL in conjunction with robotics. On the other hand, Busoniu et al. (2008) focused on multiagent reinforcement learning in their overview. Their research is referred to in this thesis as well (see section 5.5).

The closest related papers to this thesis are Mousavi et al. (2016), Li (2017) and Arulkumaran et al. (2017). These research papers are temporally very close and have therefore very similar content and structure to each other and this thesis. Whereas these papers go more into the *width* of RL, this thesis focuses on a few relevant papers with more detail.

Other content that is very closely related to this thesis is the talk given by David Silver in 2016 at an ICML conference (Silver, 2016)[1]. The structure of this thesis is in part derived from his talk and it has greatly influenced this thesis as it served as a great starting point for this thesis.

---

[1]http://techtalks.tv/talks/deep-reinforcement-learning/62360/, accessed on 3.1.2018

2.2 Research Conduction

As already mentioned, the starting point of this research was the talk by David Silver in 2016 (see footnote). Since he is a researcher at Google's DeepMind, their website[2] was used to search for more research papers. The arXiv[3] database and Google Scholar[4] were also used to search for more papers, while primarily focusing on the most recent ones. These include research papers as early as 2015 and 2016.

Besides Google's DeepMind, other big companies' artificial intelligence (AI) research departments were searched for relevant papers. These include UberAI[5], the non-profit organization OpenAI[6] and Microsoft's AI research[7]. To be informed, whenever new research papers were released, the reinforcement learning subreddit[8] was followed. When the initial number of papers were found, their relevance for this thesis was determined, based on their content, results, connection to prior work and the novelty of their work. The papers that were deemed relevant for this thesis were then thoroughly studied and their content reviewed here.

---

[2] https://deepmind.com/ - Accessed on 4.1.2018
[3] https://arxiv.org/ - Accessed on 4.1.2018
[4] https://scholar.google.de/ - Accessed on 4.1.2018
[5] http://uber.ai/ - Accessed on 4.1.2018
[6] https://openai.com/ - Accessed on 4.1.2018
[7] https://www.microsoft.com/en-us/research/lab/microsoft-research-ai/ - Accessed on 4.1.2018
[8] https://www.reddit.com/r/reinforcementlearning/ - Accessed on 4.1.2018

3 Background

This chapter is dedicated to deliver necessary background knowledge in both RL and DL in order to understand subsequent sections. The first half of this chapter will cover some of the fundamental aspects of RL and serve as an introduction into the field. That section's structure and content are based on Sutton and Barto (2017). The second half will deal with DL.

3.1 Reinforcement Learning

A typical RL model is composed of two main components, namely the agent and the environment. The agent perceives the environment and receives an observation of the current state of the environment as an input. Based on what the agent observed, it will output some action that can change the environment. The value of that change is communicated to the agent via a scalar reward. High positive values indicate that the previously chosen action led the agent closer to its goal while negative rewards punish the agent for wrong actions (Kaelbling et al., 1996, p. 237-238). The goal of the agent is to pick a series of actions that will eventually lead to the highest possible rewards. In other words, the agent has to *plan* over a long time period (e.g. the agent could take a series of seemingly *bad* actions, which could after many timesteps lead to a high reward).

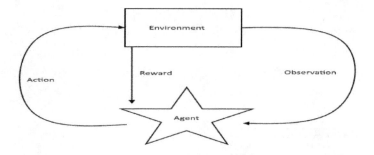

Figure 1: RL model, simplified adaptation from (Arulkumaran et al., 2017, p. 3)

The behavior of the agent is called the agent's *policy* (Sutton and Barto, 2017, p. 5) and is one of the major components in RL. It can be seen as the mapping from a certain state to a particular action. For example, the policy of an agent in a rock-paper-scissors environment could be to always pick rock.

3.1.1 Markov Decision Process

Whereas the previous section described RL conceptually, this section will introduce Markov decision processes (MDP), which are commonly used to formally describe RL problems. As can be seen in figure 1, the agent receives both an observation and a reward at every timestep. The observation is the representation of the environment's current state and will be denoted as $S_t \in S$ and the output of the agent, i.e. the action it chooses, will be denoted as $A_t \in A$. After executing an action, the reward signal R_{t+1} arrives at the agent (Sutton and Barto, 2017, p. 37-38).

Every state in an MDP must satisfy the Markov property, which states:

$$P[S_{t+1}|S_t] = P[S_{t+1}|S_1, S_2, ..., S_t]. \tag{3.1}$$

The probability of transitioning to the next state given the current state is the same as transitioning to next state given all the previous states. In other words, the current state fully characterizes the history of previous states (Silver, 2015, slide 4).

As already mentioned in 3.1, the goal of the agent is to maximize the rewards it gets over time. This goal will be written as

$$G_t = R_{t+1} + \gamma R_{t+2} + \gamma^2 R_{t+3} + ... = \sum_{k=0}^{\infty} \gamma^k R_{t+k+1} \tag{3.2}$$

where $\gamma \in [0, 1]$ is a discount factor and k in the sum is the number of timesteps (Sutton and Barto, 2017, p. 43). The closer γ is to 1 the more farsighted the agent becomes. Similarly, if γ is close to 0, the agent becomes shortsighted and is only interested in the immediate reward.

The last piece of a MDP is the state transition probability matrix. It describes the probability of transitioning to the next state s' given the current state s and the action

a the agent took (Sutton and Barto, 2017, p. 38). It is defined as

$$P_{ss'}^a = P[S_{t+1} = s' | S_t = s, A_t = a].$$ (3.3)

These components make up a MDP as a 5-tuple $\langle S, A, P, R, \gamma \rangle$, where S and A are each a set of states and actions respectively, P is the transition probability matrix, R is the reward signal and $\gamma \in [0, 1]$ is the discount factor.

Actions are chosen according to the agent's policy π, which is a mapping from states to actions (Sutton and Barto, 2017, p. 45-46) and is defined as

$$\pi(a|s) = P[A_t = a | S_t = s].$$ (3.4)

3.1.2 Value Functions

The state value function is used to define the expected total reward of being in a particular state and following the policy π. The state value function v will be written as

$$v_\pi(s) = \mathbb{E}_\pi[G_t | S_t = s],$$ (3.5)

where $\mathbb{E}[\cdot]$ is the expectation of the random input variables (Sutton and Barto, 2017, p. 46). Similarly, the value of taking a certain action in a state and then following the policy afterwards is called the state-action value q (Sutton and Barto, 2017, p. 46). It is written as

$$q(s, a) = \mathbb{E}_\pi[G_t | S_t = s, A_t = a].$$ (3.6)

These functions can both be estimated from experience. Both the state value and the state-action value function can be rewritten in a recursive manner using equation 3.2, resulting in the Bellman equations for v (Sutton and Barto, 2017, p. 46)

$$
\begin{aligned}
v_\pi(s) &= \mathbb{E}_\pi[G_t|S_t = s] \\
&= \mathbb{E}_\pi[R_{t+1} + \gamma R_{t+2} + \gamma^2 R_{t+3} + \cdots |S_t = s] \\
&= \mathbb{E}_\pi[R_{t+1} + \gamma(R_{t+2} + \gamma R_{t+3} + \cdots)|S_t = s] \\
&= \mathbb{E}_\pi[R_{t+1} + \gamma G_{t+1}|S_t = s] \\
&= \mathbb{E}_\pi[R_{t+1} + \gamma v_\pi(S_{t+1})|S_t = s]
\end{aligned}
\tag{3.7}
$$

and similarly

$$
q_\pi(s,a) = \mathbb{E}_\pi[R_{t+1} + \gamma q_\pi(S_{t+1}, A_{t+1})|S_t = s, A_t = a].
\tag{3.8}
$$

With these functions, it is possible to express the advantage of an action as

$$
A_\pi(s,a) = Q_\pi(s,a) - V_\pi(s).
\tag{3.9}
$$

In any MDP there exists atleast one optimal policy π_*. Finding π_* is the goal of the RL agent. A policy π is better than some other policy π', i.e. $\pi \geq \pi'$, if $v_\pi(s) \geq v_{\pi'}(s), \forall s \in S$. Following the optimal policy π_* will yield the highest possible reward for every state. From this, it results that the optimal value functions are

$$
v_*(s) = \max_\pi v_\pi(s), \forall s \in S
\tag{3.10}
$$

and

$$
q_*(s,a) = \max_\pi q_\pi(s,a), \forall s \in S, a \in A
\tag{3.11}
$$

(Sutton and Barto, 2017, p. 49). Since the value of state s is the same as taking the best action and following the optimal policy afterwards, it can be written as

$$
\begin{aligned}
v_*(s) &= \max_{a \in A(s)} q_{\pi_*}(s, a) \\
&= \max_{a \in A(s)} \mathbb{E}_{\pi_*}[G_t | S_t = s, A_t = a] \\
&= \max_{a \in A(s)} \mathbb{E}_{\pi_*}[R_{t+1} + \gamma G_{t+1} | S_t = s, A_t = a] \\
&= \max_{a \in A(s)} \mathbb{E}_{\pi_*}[R_{t+1} + \gamma v_*(S_{t+1}) | S_t = s, A_t = a],
\end{aligned}
\tag{3.12}
$$

where the equation above is the Bellman optimality equation for the state value. Similarly, the Bellman optimality equation for the state-action value function can be written as

$$
q_*(s, a) = \mathbb{E}[R_{t+1} + \gamma \max_{a'} q_*(S_{t+1}, a') | S_t = s, A_t = a]
\tag{3.13}
$$

(Sutton and Barto, 2017, p. 50). Having either the optimal state value or the state-action value function will solve the MDP, because it is possible to derive the optimal policy from them. If the agent knew the optimal state-action value function, for example, then executing the action with the highest q value would be the optimal behavior.

So far, only certain components of a MDP have been defined and the goal was specified. However, it was not described how to approach the goal of computing the optimal policy in an algorithmic manner. In fact, expressing v and R as a vector and substituting the expectation for the probability transition matrix, the Bellman equation can be written as:

$$
\begin{aligned}
\mathcal{I}v &= R + \gamma P v \\
\mathcal{I}v - \gamma P v &= R \\
(\mathcal{I} - \gamma P)v &= R \\
v &= (\mathcal{I} - \gamma \mathcal{P})^{-1} R,
\end{aligned}
$$

where $\mathcal{I}$ is the identity matrix. However, due to the immense computational cost of $O(n^3)$ for matrix inversion for every state n, scaling is out of the question (Silver, 2015, slide 22-23).

Using dynamic programming (DP), however, it is possible to arrive at the optimal policy iteratively. This will be covered in the next section.

3.1.3 Tabular Solution Methods

Before presenting the most recent advancements in RL that mostly include some sort of function approximator, it is necessary to view the tabular solution methods first.

Dynamic Programming

If a perfect representation, i.e. model, of the environment is given, then DP can be applied to iteratively solve for the optimal behavior (Sutton and Barto, 2017, p. 57). There are two general approaches to this, which will both be covered in this section:

1. Policy Iteration

2. Value Iteration

Policy iteration consists of two repeating steps, which are policy evaluation (prediction) and policy improvement (Sutton and Barto, 2017, p. 62).

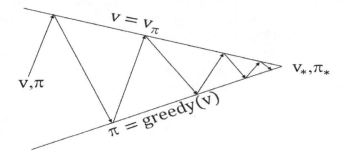

Figure 2: Policy iteration scheme, adapted from (Sutton and Barto, 2017, p. 68)

During the first step, policy evaluation, the value function v for following the current policy is computed. As mentioned above, this could (theoretically) be immediately computed but is very computationally expensive.

Using the Bellman equation, an iterative update can be defined as

$$v_{k+1}(s) := \mathbb{E}_\pi[R_{t+1} + \gamma v_k(S_{t+1})|S_t = s] \qquad \text{(Using 3.7)}$$
$$= \sum_a \pi(a|s) \sum_{s'} P_{ss'}^a \left[R_{ss'}^a + \gamma v_k(s') \right] \qquad \text{Replacing the expectation,} \qquad (3.14)$$

where $R_{ss'}^a$ is the reward received when transitioning from state s to s' by taking action a and k is the current evaluation iteration. This produces a sequence of value functions in the form of

$$v_k \to v_{k+1} \to v_{k+2} \to \cdots \to v_\pi,$$

starting with $k = 0$. This update sequence will eventually converge to the current policy that is being evaluated. In other words, by iteratively applying the equation 3.14 the quality of the policy π can be measured (Sutton and Barto, 2017, p. 58-59). All that is left is to improve the policy in the next step after its evaluation.

Policy improvement is the next step for the policy iteration scheme (Sutton and Barto, 2017, p. 60-62). The goal of this step is to *somehow* find a better policy than before, i.e. to find a policy $\pi' \geq \pi$. After the evaluation step, the value of all states are available. Suppose that a single state $s_{random} \in S$ is randomly chosen among the available states. The current value of this state, while following the current policy, is given by $v_\pi(s_{random})$. Now, suppose that for this single state, the policy is not followed for the first action. Instead of choosing an action like $a = \pi(a|s)$, the agent now looks at all the possible actions and executes the one with the highest q value and *then* follows the original policy. In other words,

$$\pi'(s_{random}) = \arg\max_a q_\pi(s_{random}, a). \qquad (3.15)$$

This is never decrease the overall performance. If the agent chooses an action that is for a fact the best action for that state, then (unless it already was the best action) the overall improvement must improve (or remain the same if it was already the best action). This process is referred to as *acting greedily*. If for a single state this greedy action improves (or stays at) the current performance, then naturally, applying it to all states improves the performance even further. If two subsequent policies return the same values for all states, i.e. $\pi' = \pi$, then both of them must be π_*. The pseudocode below shows the policy iteration scheme.

Algorithm 1 Policy Iteration, adapted from (Sutton and Barto, 2017, p. 63)

1: Initialize $V(s) \in \mathbb{R}$ and $\pi(s) \in A(s)$ arbitrarily for all $s \in S$ and $\Delta \leftarrow 0$ and θ as a small positive integer
2: **while** $\Delta < \theta$ **do**   ▷ Policy Evaluation
3:     $\Delta \leftarrow 0$
4:     **for** each $s \in S$ **do**
5:         $v \leftarrow V(s)$
6:         $V(s) \leftarrow \sum_{s'} P_{ss'}^{\pi(s)} \left[R_{ss'}^{\pi(s)} + \gamma V(s') \right]$
7:         $\Delta \leftarrow \max(\Delta, |v - V(s)|)$
8:     **end for**
9: **end while**
10: $policy\_stable \leftarrow true$
11: **for** each $s \in S$ **do**   ▷ Policy Improvement
12:     $old\_action \leftarrow \pi(s)$
13:     $\pi(s) \leftarrow \arg\max_a \sum_{s'} P_{ss'}^{a} \left[R_{ss'}^{a} + \gamma V(s') \right]$
14:     **if** $old\_action \neq \pi(s)$ **then**
15:         $policy\_stable \leftarrow false$
16:     **end if**
17: **end for**
18: **if** $policy\_stable = true$ **then**
19:     Stop and return $V \approx v_*$ and $\pi \approx \pi_*$
20: **else**
21:     Go to line 2
22: **end if**

Value Iteration

As mentioned previously, policy iteration consists of policy evaluation and improvement, where the policy evaluation step makes several loops over the entire state space.

Value iteration, on the other hand, combines policy evaluation and improvement in one update step (Sutton and Barto, 2017, p. 65-66). Instead of looping over the state space multiple times, each state is updated only once per iteration, while using

$$v_{k+1}(s) := \max_a \mathbb{E}[R_{t+1} + \gamma v_k(S_{t+1})|S_t = s, A_t = a]$$
$$= \max_a \sum_{s' \in S} P^a_{ss'}[R^a_{ss'} + \gamma v_k(s')], \tag{3.16}$$

as an update step, where the notation is the same as previously.
The value iteration algorithm is shown below.

Algorithm 2 Value Iteration, adapted from (Sutton and Barto, 2017, p. 65)

1: Initialize threshold $\theta > 0$, $\Delta \leftarrow 0$ $V(s)$ for every state arbitrarily, except $V(terminal) = 0$
2: **while** $\Delta < \theta$ **do**
3:     $\Delta \leftarrow 0$
4:     **for** $s \in S$ **do**
5:         $v \leftarrow V(s)$
6:         $V(s) \leftarrow \max_a \sum_{s' \in S} P^a_{ss'} + [R^a_{ss'} + \gamma V(s')]$
7:         $\Delta \leftarrow \max(\Delta, |v - V(s)|)$
8:     **end for**
9: **end while**
10: Output: deterministic policy $\pi \approx \pi_*$, such that

$$\pi(s) = \arg\max_a \sum_{s' \in S} P^a_{ss'}[R^a_{ss'} + \gamma V(s')]$$

Model-Free Tabular Methods

The previous section showed two methods of how to solve finite MDPs using DP. However, there were some very unrealistic assumptions so far. To use DP it is necessary to have a perfect representation of the environment. Additionally, all the possible actions must be available, which is, although difficult, a certainly more realistic assumption. On top of this, however, the state transition probabilities must also be known.

These components are rarely available for many of the modern problems and as such, other methods were needed that did not require any model, but rather relied on experience only.

These tabular model-free methods will, however, not be covered in this thesis, as they would require an entire thesis on their own. Since most of the algorithms in section 4 do not require a model of the environment, it was deemed necessary to show the procedure, when such a model was given.

3.2 Deep Learning

In this section the main concepts of DL will be covered. For the purposes of this thesis, DL methods can be seen as a form of non-linear function approximator. DL methods are a subclass of representation learning, which in turn focuses on extracting the necessary features for the task (e.g. classification or detection) (Lecun et al., 2015, p. 436).

Typically, supervised learning, which this section will be focused on, is used. Here, labeled training data is fed to a non-linear function approximator, such as a neural network. In this context, "labeled" means that along with the data (e.g. pixel values of an image) a target is also given (e.g. the image shows a dog). The network now learns a function that maps the inputs (e.g. the pixels) to the output (e.g. the label). The goal of the network is, given enough training data, to be able to generalize to new, unseen data (Lecun et al., 2015, p. 436-438).

The most widely used model architectures are feedforward (neural) networks (FNN), which are also called multilayer perceptrons (MLP) (Goodfellow et al., 2016, p. 167).

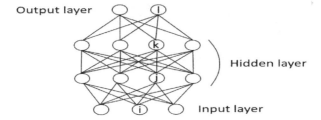

Figure 3: Deep Neural Network Example, adapted from (Lecun et al., 2015, p. 437). Indices show the corresponding neuron (e.g. i^{th} neuron of the input layer).

The architecture of these networks typically consist of multiple layers: the input layer, (multiple) hidden layers and the output layer (Lecun et al., 2015, p. 436-438), where each subsequent hidden layer can be seen as a more abstract representation of the input than the previous layer.

The structure of the network is loosely inspired by nature, particularly the model of human brains (Goodfellow et al., 2016, p. 168). Each layer consists of multiple *neurons* (which are sometimes referred to as *units*) that are connected to the *neurons* of the next layer by *weights* (see figure 3). Each weight holds some numerical value and influences the output. More formally, the mapping from input to output can be described as

$$\underbrace{y}_{\text{output}} = f(\overbrace{x}^{\text{input}}; \underbrace{\theta}_{\text{parameters}}) \tag{3.17}$$

(Goodfellow et al., 2016, p. 167). Throughout the rest of this thesis, whenever a function involves "; θ", unless specified explicitly, it can be expected to use some function approximator with parameters θ. These parameters are most of the time used to represent the values held by the weights.

So far, the components of the FNN were only mentioned. The question remains how these components interact to be able to learn a reasonable function for input-output mapping.

Most FNN are optimized with a technique called *stochastic gradient descent* (SGD), using *backpropagation* to compute the gradient of the cost function (Lecun et al., 2015, p. 437-439). The computation of the gradient involves two steps: a *forward* and a *backward* pass.

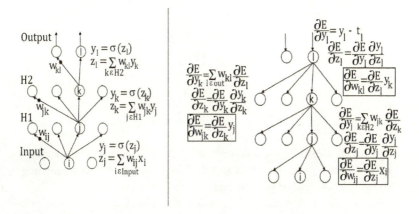

Figure 4: Forward and Backward, adapted from (Lecun et al., 2015, p. 437), some connections are omitted to preserve simplicity; t_l is the target value, E is the error function and the indices refer to the particular *neuron* in the layer.

During the forward pass, the weighted sum of the input layers are calculated. Afterwards, a non-linear function $\sigma(\cdot)$ is applied to the weighted sum[9]. Usually, a rectified linear unit $\sigma(z) = \max(0, z)$ is used, although other non-linear functions are possible as well (Lecun et al., 2015, p. 437-438). This is shown on the left side of figure 4, where w_{ab} are the weights from neurons in layer a to layer b.

After the forward pass, the cost function is computed. This is usually the squared difference between the output of the output layer and the target value. This can be multiplied by 0.5 to make differentiating easier. In other words, $0.5(y_l - t)^2$, where y_l is the output of the last layer. Now that the cost, i.e. the difference from the expected output and the networks output is known, the question is how to adjust the weights such that the output matches more closely the target.

For this, the change in the cost function with respect to all the weights must be calcu-

---

[9]Normally, a *bias* is added to this sum (Lecun et al., 2015, p. 437), which will be disregarded here for the sake of simplicity.

lated. For the specific network in figure 4, it would have the form

$$\nabla E = \begin{bmatrix} \frac{\partial E}{\partial w_{kl}} \\ \\ \frac{\partial E}{\partial w_{jk}} \\ \\ \frac{\partial E}{\partial w_{ij}} \end{bmatrix} \tag{3.18}$$

Adjusting the weights in the opposite direction of ∇E will adjust the weights to minimize the cost function (Lecun et al., 2015, p. 436). The computation of these derivatives of the cost function with respect to the weights is shown in figure 4.

Figure 3 is one of many model architectures in DL. Another important one of those models is the *convolutional (neural) network* (CNN), which has shown to be very strong in image classification (Krizhevsky et al., 2012).

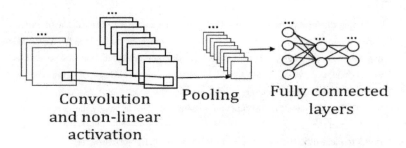

Figure 5: Convolutional neural network example, adapted and simplified from (Lecun et al., 2015, p. 438-440)

Figure 5 shows an example architecture of a CNN. The input consists of multiple dimensions of arrays (e.g. one dimension for the red-value of a pixel, one dimension for the green-value and one for the blue-value). On each of those dimensions, a *filter*[10] is applied, which is kept fixed for the entire input (Lecun et al., 2015, p. 439). This step is called *convolution.* Mathematically, it can be written as

$$x_{ij}^l = \sum_{p=0}^{k-1} \sum_{q=0}^{k-1} w_{pq} \; y_{i+p,j+q}^{l-1}, \qquad (3.19)$$

where i and j are the indices of the the neuron, w_{pq} is a filter with dimensions $k \times k$, the superscript l is the current layer and $y_{x,y}^{l-1}$ is the output of the neuron of the previous layer with the indices x, y (Nielsen, 2015, chapter 6).

After the convolution, a non-linear activation function is applied, which is typically a rectified linear unit

$$y_{ij}^l = \sigma(x_{ij}^l), \qquad (3.20)$$

where $\sigma(\cdot) = \max(0, \cdot)$ (Nielsen, 2015, chapter 6). Usually, a *pooling step* is used afterwards, where, in the case of *max* pooling, the highest value of a certain region is chosen for the next layer. These blocks, i.e. convolution and pooling, can be repeated multiple times and in any order (Lecun et al., 2015, p. 438-439). At the end of the *CNN* multiple fully connected layers exist (Lecun et al., 2015, p. 439), which have the same structure as seen in 3.

Same as with the previous network, this one can also be trained using SGD. Although the backpropagation in CNN is similar to the previous case, the details will be omitted here.

---

[10]Throughout the literature, there were several names for this used interchangeably: *feature map, kernel, weights, filter* and more. Conceptually, one can imagine the input as a big painting and the feature map as a flashlight that points on a certain field of the picture. That field is the *receptive field* of the neuron of the next layer.

4 Results

This chapter will be divided into two parts: firstly value-based approaches and secondly policy-based approaches. Furthermore, the findings within this chapter will be primarily focused on the algorithms and the results of their experiments, which will be presented at the end of this chapter, when all the algorithms were introduced.

The third approach in RL is the model-based approach. However, because they are very little researched, their coverage must wait until chapter 5, where open research questions are discussed.

4.1 Value-Based Deep Reinforcement Learning

The first half of this chapter is dedicated to value-based approaches in DRL. Value-based approaches aim to find the Q-function, which can be used to derive the optimal policy (see section 3.1.2).

4.1.1 Deep Q-Learning and Deep Q-Networks

One of the earliest major achievements in DRL was the invention of the value-based approach of Deep Q-Networks (Mnih et al., 2013, 2015). On several Atari 2600 games (Bellemare et al., 2012) the Deep Q-Network (DQN) algorithm was capable of achieving super-human performance (Mnih et al., 2015, p. 531). The authors used a deep CNN to approximate the optimal action-value function (see section 3.1.2), such that $Q(s, a; \theta) \approx Q^*(s, a)$, where θ are the weights of the CNN. Such a neural network is referred to as a Q-network by the authors (Mnih et al., 2015, p. 529).

As input, the agent receives only the current game screen $x_t \in \mathbb{R}^d$ as a vector of pixel values and the according game score as a reward signal. Because it is impossible to derive the entire situation from only a single frame of the game screen, Mnih et al. (2015) store sequences of actions and observations $s_t = x_1, a_1, x_2, \ldots, a_{t-1}, x_t$.[11]

The DQN algorithm uses two concepts: experience replay (Lin, 1993, p. 29) and updates

---

[11]For example, in the game of Breakout it is unclear whether the ball is either moving up or down, given only one single game frame.

towards a periodically updated target network, which is a significant factor for increased stability (Mnih et al., 2015, p. 529).

To perform the experience replay technique, the state transitions experienced by the agent are stored as $e_t = (s_t, a_t, r_t, s_{t+1})$ into a *replay memory* $D_t = \{e_1, \ldots, e_t\}$ over which random minibatches are uniformly sampled, i.e. $(s, a, r, s') \sim U(D)$ (Mnih et al., 2015, p. 529). One of the advantages of experience replay is the increased data efficiency due to possible multiple uses of experiences. Because experience replay randomly samples batches of experience, the variance of learning updates is reduced, which increases learning performance (Mnih et al., 2015, p. 535).

The Q-network was trained by minimizing the following series of loss functions $L_i(\theta_i)$ at every iteration i

$$L_i(\theta_i) = \mathbb{E}_{s,a,r,s'} \big[\big(\underbrace{r + \gamma \max_{a'} Q(s', a'; \theta_i^-)}_{\text{approx. target action-value}} - \overbrace{Q(s, a; \theta_i)}^{\text{action-value}} \big)^2 \big], \tag{4.1}$$

where θ_i^- are the parameters of previous iterations, which are updated every C time steps (Mnih et al., 2015, p. 529). Differentiating the loss function above with respect to the weights, Mnih et al. (2015) get the following gradient

$$\nabla_{\theta_i} L(\theta_i) = \mathbb{E}_{s,a,r,s'} \left[\left(r + \gamma \max_{a'} Q(s', a'; \theta_i^-) - Q(s, a; \theta_i) \right) \nabla_{\theta_i} Q(s, a; \theta_i) \right]. \tag{4.2}$$

To reduce the high input dimensions of raw Atari 2600 game frames, Mnih et al. (2015) use a preprocessing function $\phi(s_t)$, which shrinks the input images to more manageable sizes. The details of that function will be skipped, since it is not part of the logic of the DQN. The algorithm below shows this approach

---

Algorithm 3 Deep Q-Learning with Experience replay, adapted from (Mnih et al., 2015, p. 535)

1: Initialize replay memory D to capacity N
2: Initialize action-value function Q with random weights θ
3: Initialize target action value function $\hat{Q}$ with weights $\theta^- = \theta$
4: **for** $episode = 1, M$ **do**
5:     Initialize sequence $s_1 = \{x_1\}$ and preprocessed sequence $\phi_1 = \phi(s_1)$
6:     **for** $t = 1, T$ **do**
7:         Select a random action a_t with probability ε
8:         otherwise select $a_t = arg\max_a Q(\phi(s_t), a; \theta)$
9:         Execute action a_t in emulator and observe reward r_t and image x_{t+1}
10:       Set $s_{t+1} = s_t, a_t, x_{t+1}$ and preprocess $\phi_{t+1} = \phi(s_{t+1})$
11:       Store transition $(\phi_t, a_t, r_t, \phi_{t+1})$ in D
12:       Sample random minibatch of transitions $(\phi_j, a_j, r_j, \phi_{j+1})$ from D
13:       Set $y_j = \begin{cases} r_j & \text{if episode terminates at step j+1} \\ r_j + \gamma \max_{a'} \hat{Q}(\phi_{j+1}, a'; \theta^-) & \text{otherwise} \end{cases}$
14:       Perform a gradient descent step on $(y_j - Q(\phi_j, a_j; \theta))^2$ w.r.t. θ
15:       Every C steps reset $\hat{Q} = Q$
16:     **end for**
17: **end for**

Since the introduction of the DQN algorithm there have been several extension over the years, which will be covered in later sections. See section 4.3 for the performance of DQN.

4.1.2 Double Q-Learning and Double Q-Network

One of the problems of the standard Q-learning algorithm (Watkins and Dayan, 1992; Watkins, 1989) is the overestimation of certain action-values, as shown by Thrun and Schwartz (1993). The upper bound of the average overestimation in Q-learning is $\gamma \varepsilon \frac{n-1}{n+1}$ (Thrun and Schwartz, 1993, p. 3), where n represents the number of available actions and ε in the interval $[-\varepsilon; \varepsilon]$ are the evenly distributed random errors within the action-values and γ is the discount factor.

However, should every action-value be uniformly overestimated, the overall policy would not be effected, since the relative difference would remain the same (van Hasselt et al., 2015, p. 1). The DQN algorithm from the previous section 4.1.1 suffers from several overestimations, as demonstrated by van Hasselt et al. (2015). They proposed the usage of double Q-learning (van Hasselt, 2010) in conjunction with DQN (Mnih et al., 2015) to resolve that issue.

Double Q-learning uses two action-value functions, Q^A and Q^B, where one function is used as a target for the other, while the other chooses the greedy policy (van Hasselt, 2010, p. 4). Since both functions are updated using different sets of experience, the difference between the target value from one function and the action value from the other function can be seen as an unbiased estimate for the actual value of the action. The double Q-learning algorithm is depicted below.

Algorithm 4 Double Q-Learning, adapted from (van Hasselt, 2010, p. 5)

1: Initialize Q^A,Q^B,s
2: **repeat**
3:     Choose a, based on $Q^A(s,\cdot)$ and $Q^B(s,\cdot)$, observe r, s'
4:     Choose (e.g. randomly) either UPDATE(A) or UPDATE(B)
5:     **if** UPDATE(A) **then**
6:         Define $a^* = \arg\max_a Q^A(s', a)$
7:         $Q^A(s,a) \leftarrow Q^A(s,a) + \alpha(s,a)(r + \gamma Q^B(s',a^*) - Q^A(s,a))$
8:     **else if** UPDATE(B) **then**
9:         Define $b^* = \arg\max_a Q^B(s', a)$
10:      $Q^B(s,a) \leftarrow Q^B(s,a) + \alpha(s,a)(r + \gamma Q^A(s',a^*) - Q^B(s,a))$
11:     **end if**
12:    $s \leftarrow s'$
13: **until** end

DQN already consists of two value functions. For the double DQN algorithm, the greedy policy is evaluated by the online network, i.e. Q with weights θ, while its value is estimated by the target network, i.e. $\hat{Q}$ with weights θ^- (van Hasselt et al., 2015, p. 4). Double DQN shows great similarity to the original DQN. However, the double DQN algorithm differs only from algorithm 3 regarding the target value. The target value from algorithm 3 in line 13 is replaced by

$$Y_t^{DoubleDQN} \equiv R_{t+1} + \gamma Q(S_{t+1}, \arg\max_a Q(S_{t+1}, a; \theta_t), \theta_t^-). \tag{4.3}$$

4.1.3 Prioritized Replay

The previous section 4.1.1 introduced DQN (Mnih et al., 2013, 2015), which utilized the experience replay technique (Lin, 1993) to increase the agent's performance. The motivation for using experience replay was to increase learning efficiency by breaking the strong correlations between consecutive samples as was shown by (Mnih et al., 2015). However, some experiences have a greater influence on the learning progress than others, which is the motivation behind prioritized experience replay (Schaul et al., 2015). Assuming it is known which experiences to store, Schaul et al. (2015) proposed a method for selecting the significant experiences to be replayed.

One possibility to measure the importance of experiences is to use the temporal difference (TD) error[12] δ in transitions, which indicates how unanticipated the transition was to the agent. Contrary to the uniform random sampling from the standard experience replay method (see algorithm 3, line 12), Schaul et al. (2015) utilize a stochastic sampling method. They define the probability of sampling the transition i from the experience replay memory as

$$P(i) = \frac{p_i^\alpha}{\sum_k p_k^\alpha}, \tag{4.4}$$

where $p_i > 0$ is the priority of the transition i, k is the size of the minibatch (see algorithm 5) and α is an indication of how much prioritization is used (Schaul et al., 2015, p. 3-4). For p_i the authors show two possibilities:

1. Direct and proportional prioritization approach $p_i = |\delta| + \epsilon$, where ϵ is a small positive number to prevent the memory from not being visited should the error reach zero.

2. Rank-based approach $p_i = \frac{1}{rank(i)}$, where $rank(i)$ is the rank of transition in the replay memory after being sorted according to the TD error $|\delta_i|$.

The second approach is preferred due to higher apparent robustness (Schaul et al., 2015, p. 4). To counteract the bias introduced by the prioritized replay technique, the authors

---

[12]See the appendix in (Schaul et al., 2015) for alternative measures.

use importance-sampling (IS) weights as

$$w_i = \left(\frac{1}{N} \cdot \frac{1}{P(i)}\right)^\beta, \tag{4.5}$$

where β linearly approaches 1 as learning comes to an end. Furthermore, IS is stabilized by $\frac{1}{max_i w_i}$. The algorithm below shows this approach for the double DQN (D-DQN) algorithm.

Algorithm 5 D-DQN:Proportional Prioritization, adapted from (Schaul et al., 2015, p. 5)

1: **Input:** minibatch k, step-size η, replay period K and size N, exponents α and β, budget T
2: Initialize replay memory $\mathcal{H} = \emptyset$, $\Delta = 0$, $p_1 = 1$
3: Observe S_0 and choose $A_0 \sim \pi_\theta(S_0)$
4: **for** $t = 1$ **to** T **do**
5:     Observe S_t, R_t, γ_t
6:     Store transition $(S_{t-1}, A_{t-1}, R_t, \gamma_t, S_t)$ in $\mathcal{H}$ with maximal priority $p_t = max_{i<t}p_i$
7:     **if** $t \equiv 0 \mod K$ **then**
8:         **for** $j = 1$ **to** k **do**
9:             Sample transition $j \sim P(j) = p_j^\alpha / \sum_i p_i^\alpha$
10:             Compute importance-sampling weight $w_j = (N \cdot P(j))^{-\beta} / \max_i w_i$
11:             Compute TD error $\delta_j = R_j + \gamma_j Q_{target}(S_j, \arg\max_a Q(S_j, a)) - Q(S_{j-1}, A_{j-1})$
12:             Update transition priority $p_j \leftarrow |\delta_j|$
13:             Accumulate weight-change $\Delta \leftarrow \Delta + w_j \cdot \delta_j \cdot \Delta_\theta Q(S_{j-1}, A_{j-1})$
14:         **end for**
15:         Update weights $\theta \leftarrow \theta + \eta \cdot \Delta$, reset $\Delta = 0$
16:         From time to time copy weights into target network $\theta_{target} \leftarrow \theta$
17:     **end if**
18:     Choose action $A_t \sim \pi_\theta(S_t)$
19: **end for**

This algorithm achieved better performance on 41 out of 49 Atari 2600 games when compared to DQN (see section 4.3).

4.1.4 Dueling Network

In some RL tasks, there can be states, where estimating the action-values for every possible action is unnecessary. This is especially relevant for situations, where certain actions exist that do not have any significant effect on the environment. This is the motivation behind the dueling network architecture (Wang et al., 2015). The figure below shows the novel architecture design.

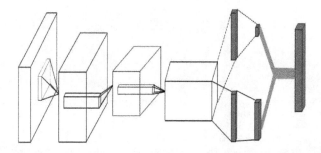

Figure 6: Dueling Network Architecture, adapted from (Wang et al., 2015, p. 1)

The network consists of two halves: the first part is a CNN, as it was used in DQN (Mnih et al., 2015) and the second part, which incorporates two streams that are fully connected to the last layer of the CNN (Wang et al., 2015, p. 4).
One of the streams estimates the state-value $V(s; \theta, \beta)$, where θ are the parameters of the CNN and β are the parameters of this stream. Similarly, the other stream returns an estimate for the advantage of an action $A(s, a; \theta, \alpha)$, where α are the parameters of this particular stream. These two streams are combined to produce a collection of Q values (Wang et al., 2015, p. 4), making it possible to train this network with already known approaches such as double DQN.
Wang et al. (2015) proposed two variants for combining these two streams. Either

$$Q(s, a; \theta, \alpha, \beta) = V(s; \theta, \beta) + \left(A(s, a; \theta, \alpha) - \max_{a' \in |A|} A(s, a'; \theta, \alpha)\right) \qquad (4.6)$$

or instead of using the max operator and averaging instead

$$Q(s, a; \theta, \alpha, \beta) = V(s; \theta, \beta) + \left(A(s, a; \theta, \alpha) - \frac{1}{|A|} \sum_{a'} A(s, a'; \theta, \alpha) \right). \qquad (4.7)$$

The latter approach is preferred due to better results. Once again, this algorithm was tested on the Atari 2600 testbed and showed improvements compared to previous attempts (see section 4.3).

4.1.5 Distributional Reinforcement Learning

Bellemare et al. (2017) investigate in their work the importance of value distributions in RL. The value distribution is the probability distribution of the random returns an agent can receive through the interaction with its environment. This is different from other approaches, where the expected value is computed and not a whole value distribution. More specifically, this value distribution Z is be defined as

$$Z(s, a) \overset{D}{=} R(s, a) + \gamma Z(S', A'). \qquad (4.8)$$

Equation 4.8 is the distributional Bellman equation[13] (Bellemare et al., 2017, p. 1) and appears very similar to the *regular* equations that were already shown in section 3.1.2. However, here, not an expected value is described, but a whole distribution of values. Furthermore, Bellemare et al. (2017) defined the distributional Bellman operator $\mathcal{T}^\pi$, which will later be used to evaluate the current policy π, as

$$\mathcal{T}^\pi Z(s, a) \overset{D}{:=} R(s, a) + \gamma P^\pi Z(s, a), \qquad (4.9)$$

where P^π are the visitation frequencies under policy π.

The value distribution is modeled as a discrete distribution by the authors, Bellemare et al. (2017). It is parameterized by $N \in \mathbb{N}$ and V_{MIN}, $V_{MAX} \in \mathbb{R}$. The support of the distribution is the set of atoms $\{z_i = V_{MIN} + i\Delta z : 0 \le i < N\}$, where $\Delta z := \frac{V_{MAX} - V_{MIN}}{N-1}$ (Bellemare et al., 2017, p. 5). Now, given some parameterized model (e.g. a neural

---

[13]The symbol $\overset{D}{=}$ verbally means *'distributed like/as'*

network, parameterized with θ), the probabilities of these atoms are predicted as

$$Z_\theta(s, a) = z_i \text{ with probability } p_i(s, a) := \frac{e^{\theta_i(s,a)}}{\sum_j e^{\theta_j(s,a)}}. \tag{4.10}$$

Because the prediction Z_θ and the Bellman update $\mathcal{T}Z_\theta$, i.e. the evaluation of Z_θ, have different supports, Kullback-Leibler (KL) divergence cannot be calculated between those distributions and, since the authors work with samples of transitions, the minimization of the Wasserstein metric[14] can also not be applied (Bellemare et al., 2017, p. 5-6).

To solve this, the authors Bellemare et al. (2017) included a projection step Φ, where the sampled Bellman update $\hat{\mathcal{T}}Z_\theta$ is projected onto the support of the predicted value distribution Z_θ. During the projection step, the Bellman update $\hat{\mathcal{T}}z_j$ is computed for every atom z_j and its probabilities $p_j(s', \pi(s'))$, where π is a greedy policy, are distributed to the closest neighboring atoms (Bellemare et al., 2017, p. 5-6). In other words, each atom i of the projected update has the value

$$(\Phi\hat{\mathcal{T}}Z_\theta(s, a))_i = \sum_{j=0}^{N-1} \left[1 - \frac{|[\mathcal{T}z_j]_{V_{MIN}}^{V_{MAX}} - z_i|}{\Delta z} \right]_0^1 p_j(s', \pi(s')), \tag{4.11}$$

where $[\cdot]_b^a$ clips its argument to be between $[a, b]$ (Bellemare et al., 2017, 5-6).

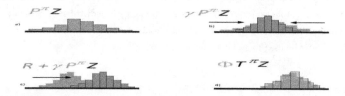

Figure 7: Distributional Bellman Operator, adapted from (Bellemare et al., 2017, p. 2): "(a) Next state distribution under policy π, (b) Discounting shrinks the distribution towards 0, (c) The reward shifts it, and (d) Projection step [...]" (Bellemare et al., 2017, p. 2)

---

[14]The details of the Wasserstein metric are omitted due to spatial reasons. See (Bellemare et al., 2017, p. 3) for more information. Very abstractly and only for the sake of this thesis, it is enough to think of it as some measure of *difference* between distributions.

Now that the projected Bellman update and the predicted distribution have the same support, the KL divergence between these two distributions can be minimized. As is the case with DQN (see section 4.1.1) the target distribution will be parameterized with a fixed parameter $\tilde{\theta}$. Finally, the KL divergence is minimized (e.g. by gradient descent)

$$D_{KL}\Big(\Phi\hat{\mathcal{T}}Z_{\tilde{\theta}}(s,a)||Z_\theta(s,a)\Big) \tag{4.12}$$

This algorithm, named *categorical algorithm* is shown below. For the number of atoms, i.e. N, 51 showed the greatest performance (Bellemare et al., 2017, p. 6-8).

Algorithm 6 Categorical Algorithm, adapted from (Bellemare et al., 2017, p. 6)

1: **input** A transition $s_t, a_t, r_t, s_{t+1}, \gamma_t \in [0,1]$
2: $Q(s_{t+1}, a) := \sum_i z_i p_i(s_{t+1}, a)$
3: $a^* \leftarrow \arg\max_a Q(s_{t+1}, a)$ $\triangleright$ Greedy policy π
4: $m_i = 0, \, i \in 0, 1, \ldots, N-1$
5: **for** $j \in 0, 1, \ldots, N-1$ **do**
6:     $\hat{\mathcal{T}}z_j \leftarrow \big[r_t + \gamma_t z_j\big]_{V_{MIN}}^{V_{MAX}}$ $\triangleright$ Compute the projection of $\hat{\mathcal{T}}z_j$ onto the support z_i
7:     $b_j \leftarrow (\hat{\mathcal{T}}z_j - V_{MIN})/\Delta z$ $\triangleright$ $b_j \in [0, N-1]$
8:     $l \leftarrow \lfloor b_j \rfloor, \, u \leftarrow \lceil b_j \rceil$
9:     $m_l \leftarrow m_l + p_j(s_{t+1}, a^*)(u - b_j)$ $\triangleright$ Distribute probability of $\hat{\mathcal{T}}z_j$
10:    $m_u \leftarrow m_u + p_j(s_{t+1}, a^*)(b_j - l)$
11: **end for**
12: **output** $-\sum_i m_i \log p_i(s_t, a_t)$ $\triangleright$ Cross-entropy loss (KL divergence)

At that time, this algorithm **vastly** outperformed any of the previous algorithms when it was tested on the Atari 2600 test suite (Bellemare et al., 2012). It also learned quicker than the other algorithms as well (see section 4.3). However, it was later trumped by the learning agent presented in the next section, called *Rainbow*. For more discussion on distributional RL, (Rowland et al., 2018) is referred to.

4.1.6 Rainbow

As of the time of this writing, the most recent and best performing RL agent was introduced by Hessel et al. (2017). This agent, henceforth only referred to as *Rainbow*, combines several achievements in the field of DRL into a single learning agent. These are

- DQN (Mnih et al., 2013, 2015)

- Distributional RL (Bellemare et al., 2017)

- Double Q-Learning (van Hasselt, 2010)

- Prioritized Experience Replay (Schaul et al., 2015)

- Dueling Networks (Wang et al., 2015)

- Multi-step Learning (Sutton, 1988)

- Noisy Nets (Fortunato et al., 2017)

Rainbow is currently the state-of-the-art RL agent. Not only does this agent **significantly** outperform any of the agents presented in this chapter (when tested on the Atari 2600 testbed), it does so also much more efficiently (see section 4.3).

4.2 Policy-Based Deep Reinforcement Learning

The previous section showed several approaches in value-based, which attempted to approximate the optimal Q-function. One other approach would be to directly find the optimal policy. These approaches will be covered in this section.

4.2.1 Asynchronous Advantage Actor-Critic

Mnih et al. (2016) proposed several methods for asynchronous reinforcement learning. The underlying idea is to run multiple agents on multiple instances of the environment in parallel (Mnih et al., 2016, p. 1). Whereas previous attempts like Gorila (Nair et al., 2015) ran several learners on multiple machines using dedicated GPU hardware, Mnih et al. (2016) ran their method on a regular multicore CPU (Mnih et al., 2016, p. 1).

Although Mnih et al. (2016) presented several asynchronous variants of RL algorithm, this section will only focus on the asynchronous advantage actor-critic method (A3C), since it performs the best among all the methods.

In A3C (Mnih et al., 2016), the actor is the parameterized policy $\pi(a_t|s_t;\theta)$, where θ are the parameters of the policy. The critic, i.e. the value function, is $V(s_t; \theta_v)$, where θ_v are the parameters of the value function. The algorithm works in the forward view, which means that it takes in the returns of the next n steps and uses these to update the policy and the value function (see algorithm 7 line 18, 19). These updates occur either when a terminal state is reached or the agent already performed t_{max} actions (Mnih et al., 2016, p. 4).

Since there are multiple learners, each of those will examine different parts of the environment. This results in a wide variety of much less correlated experiences, which in turn eradicates the need for experience replay (Mnih et al., 2016, p. 3). The A3C method is depicted in the algorithm below.

Algorithm 7 A3C, adapted from (p. 4 supplementary material of Mnih et al. (2016))

1: // *Assume global shared parameter vectors θ and θ_v and global shared counter $T = 0$*
2: // *Assume thread-specific parameter vectors θ' and θ'_v*
3: Initialize thread step counter $t \leftarrow 1$
4: **repeat**
5:     Reset gradients $d\theta \leftarrow 0$ and $d\theta'_v \leftarrow 0$
6:     Synchronize thread-specific parameters $\theta' = \theta$ and $\theta'_v = \theta_v$
7:     $t_{start} = t$
8:     Get state s_t
9:     **repeat**
10:         Perform a_t according to policy $\pi(a_t|s_t; \theta')$
11:         Receive reward r_t and new state $s_t + 1$
12:         $t \leftarrow t + 1$
13:         $T \leftarrow T + 1$
14:     **until** terminal s_t **or** $t - t_{start} == t_{max}$
15:     $R = \begin{cases} 0 & \text{for terminal } s_t \\ V(s_t, \theta'_v) & \text{for non-terminal } s_t \text{ // Bootstrap from last state} \end{cases}$
16:     **for** $i \in \{t - 1, \ldots, t_{start}\}$ **do**
17:         $R \leftarrow r_i + \gamma R$
18:         Accumulate gradients w.r.t. θ' : $d\theta \leftarrow d\theta + \Delta_{\theta'} \log \pi(a_i|s_i; \theta')(R - V(s_i; \theta'_v))$
19:         Accumulate gradients w.r.t. θ'_v : $d\theta_v \leftarrow d\theta_v + \partial(R - V(s_i; \theta'_v))^2/\partial\theta'_v$
20:     **end for**
21:     Perform asynchronous update of θ using $d\theta$ and of θ_v using $d\theta_v$
22: **until** $T > T_{max}$

This algorithm vastly outperformed previous attempts at the Atari 2600 testbed (see section 4.3). It was also tested successfully on locomotion tasks in the MuJoCo physics engine (Todorov et al., 2012).

4.2.2 Trust Region Policy Optimization

Schulman et al. (2015) "first prove that minimizing a certain surrogate objective function guarantees policy improvement with non-trivial step sizes" (Schulman et al., 2015, p. 1). The authors make some approximations to the theoretical foundation of monotonic improvement to derive a practical algorithm, which they call *trust region policy optimization* (TRPO).

For their proof Schulman et al. (2015) use a slightly simplified version of the lower bounds on the improvement of the policy performance, which can be computed using the conservative policy iteration update scheme (Kakade and Langford, 2002, p. 4-6). However, this lower bound is restricted to mixture policies, i.e. the combination of the current policy and another policy π' (Schulman et al., 2015, p. 1-3).

Schulman et al. (2015) extend this lower bound to general stochastic policies and provide an algorithm for guaranteed monotonic policy improvement using the equation below. The authors derived from their proofs that

$$\eta(\tilde{\pi}) \geq L_\pi(\tilde{\pi}) - C \cdot D_{KL}^{\max}(\pi, \tilde{\pi}), \tag{4.13}$$

with equality at $\tilde{\pi} = \pi$ (Schulman et al., 2015, p. 3). The following paragraph gives a short description as to what the components of the equation above stand for.

- $\tilde{\pi}$: Some other policy

- π: The previous policy that is being improved upon

- $\eta(\pi)$: The expected discounted reward of a policy π

- $L_\pi(\tilde{\pi})$: The local approximation of the advantage of a policy π over the other policy $\tilde{\pi}$; more specifically:

$$L_\pi(\tilde{\pi}) = \eta(\pi) + \sum_s p_\pi(s) \cdot \sum_a \tilde{\pi}(a|s) A_\pi(s, a),$$

where $p_\pi(s)$ are the (unnormalized) discounted visitation frequencies:

$$p_\pi(s) = P(s_0 = s) + \gamma P(s_1 = s) + \gamma^2 P(s_2 = s) + \cdots$$

- $D_{KL}^{\max}(\pi, \tilde{\pi})$: KL divergence[15] between π and $\tilde{\pi}$, such that

$$D_{KL}^{\max}(\pi, \tilde{\pi}) = \max_s D_{KL}\Big(\pi(\cdot|s)||\tilde{\pi}(\cdot|s)\Big)$$

- C: Penalty coefficient

$$C = \frac{4\epsilon\gamma}{(1-\gamma)^2},$$

where $\epsilon = \max_{s,a} |A_\pi(s, a)|$

If the right-hand side of equation 4.13 is maximized then the left-hand side is guaranteed to improve as well. Schulman et al. (2015) note, however, using the penalty coefficient C makes the step sizes become very small in practice. To overcome this problem, a constraint on the KL divergence was introduced, which is called the *trust region* (Schulman et al., 2015, p. 3-4).

Overloading the previous notation, such that the parameter vectors of the policies are used instead of the policy itself (e.g. $\eta(\theta) := \eta(\pi_\theta)$), Schulman et al. (2015) define

$$\bar{D}_{KL}^p(\theta_1, \theta_2) := \mathbb{E}_{s \sim p}\Big[D_{KL}(\pi_{\theta_1}(\cdot|s)||\pi_{\theta_2}(\cdot|s)) \Big], \tag{4.14}$$

where $s \sim p$ means that states are sampled according to the visitation frequencies p (Schulman et al., 2015, p. 4). Finally, Schulman et al. (2015) propose the following optimization problem, where δ is the bound on the KL divergence, to generate a policy update

$$\max_\theta L_{\theta_{old}}(\theta), \text{which is the objective}$$
$$\text{subject to } \bar{D}_{KL}^{p_{\theta_{old}}}(\theta_{old}, \theta) \leq \delta, \text{which is the constraint.} \tag{4.15}$$

---

[15]The KL divergence can, atleast for the purposes of this thesis, be seen as a measure of *difference* between distributions. The formula for computing this is $D_{KL}(P||Q) = -\sum_i P(i) \log \frac{Q(i)}{P(i)}$ for discrete distributions P and Q.

To solve this optimization problem, the objective and constraint function are approximated using Monte Carlo (MC) simulation, i.e. to run simulations and sample the trajectories of the simulations. For this, the authors expand $L_{\theta_{old}}$ and rewrite equation 4.15 in terms of expectations (Schulman et al., 2015, p. 4), resulting in

$$\max_{\theta} \mathbb{E}_{s \sim p_{\theta_{old}}, a \sim q} \left[\frac{\pi_\theta(a|s)}{q(a|s)} Q_{\theta_{old}}(s, a) \right]$$
$$\text{subject to } \mathbb{E}_{s \sim p_{\theta_{old}}} \left[D_{KL} \left(\pi_{\theta_1}(\cdot|s) || \pi_{\theta_2}(\cdot|s) \right) \right] \leq \delta. \tag{4.16}$$

The expectations and the Q-value are replaced by sample averages and empirical estimates, respectively, for which Schulman et al. (2015) propose two different sampling schemes: *single path* and *vine* (Schulman et al., 2015, p. 4-5). These schemes are illustrated in the figure below.

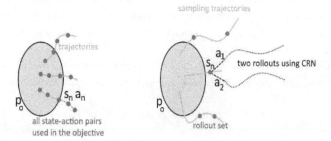

Figure 8: TRPO sampling techniques, adapted from (Schulman et al., 2015, p. 4)

In short: on the left (*single path*), a set of states are sampled and the old policy $\pi_{\theta_{old}}$ is simulated for those states, producing several trajectories. The state-action pairs generated in those simulations are then used in the objective to compute the Q-function. On the right (*vine*), initial states are sampled first. Then, using π_{θ_i}, several trajectories are generated. The rollout set is a subset of the reached states along the trajectories. For every state in the rollout set, some actions are sampled and performed (a_1, a_2 in figure 8). Then short trajectories are simulated, using common random numbers (CRN) for variance reduction (Schulman et al., 2015, p. 4-5). The practical algorithm is shown below.

Algorithm 8 Trust Region Policy Optimization, adapted from (Schulman et al., 2015, p. 5)

1: Collect a set of state-action pairs along with Monte Caro estimates of their Q-values, using either *single path* or *vine*
2: Construct the estimated objective and constraint in equation 4.16, by averaging over samples
3: Approximately solve this constrained optimization problem to update the policy's parameter vector θ ▷ For this, Schulman et al. (2015) use a conjugate gradient algorithm followed by a line search. The details of these procedures are omitted as it would otherwise go beyond the scope of this thesis.

The authors ran this algorithm on multiple testbeds. TRPO performed well in locomotion tasks, such as swimming, hopping and walking gaits using simulated robots, and performed well on Atari 2600 games (see section 4.3).

4.2.3 Deep Deterministic Policy Gradients

Lillicrap et al. (2015) proposed an actor-critic, model-free algorithm, which is structured upon the deterministic policy gradients (Silver et al., 2014). This algorithm was named Deep Deterministic Policy Gradient (D-DPG). Furthermore, it is a combination of other features that were responsible for the success of DQN (Mnih et al., 2013, 2015), namely experience replay (Lin, 1993) and a variant of target networks. Additionally, the authors Lillicrap et al. (2015) also use batch normalization (Ioffe and Szegedy, 2015).

The key differences between stochastic and deterministic policy gradients is that in the stochastic case the gradient integrates over state and action space, as opposed to the deterministic case, which only integrates over the state space. Because of this, stochastic policy gradients are computationally more expensive (Silver et al., 2014, p. 1).

As such, Silver et al. (2014) proposed an off-policy, actor-critic algorithm to learn the deterministic policy. Off-policy means that the agent explores the environment while following a stochastic behavior policy. Its goal, however, is to learn about the deterministic target policy (Silver et al., 2014, p. 1).

Lillicrap et al. (2015) extended the ideas from Silver et al. (2014). In the deterministic policy gradient (DPG) algorithm the actor chooses an action according to the deterministic policy $a = \mu_\theta(s)$, where θ is the parameter vector of the deterministic policy (Silver et al., 2014, p. 1). The parameters of the actor are then updated in the direction of the gradient such that

$$\nabla_\theta J(\mu_\theta) = \mathbb{E}_{s \sim p^\mu}\left[\nabla_\theta \mu_\theta(s) \nabla_a Q^\mu(s, a)|_{a=\mu_\theta(s)}\right], \tag{4.17}$$

where $J(\mu_\theta)$ is the performance function, i.e. the accumulated discounted reward from the start state while following the deterministic policy μ_θ and p^μ is the discounted state distribution (i.e. the state visitation frequencies) (Silver et al., 2014, p. 3-4).

As already mentioned, D-DPG uses both experience replay (Lin, 1993, p. 29) and a variant of target networks with copies Q' and μ' as the targets, whose parameters are slowly updated to keep track of what was newly learned (Lillicrap et al., 2015, p. 4). Furthermore, the feature vector of the environment may consist of values that have different units, making their range vary greatly. To address this issue Lillicrap et al. (2015) utilize batch normalization (Ioffe and Szegedy, 2015) to scale the components to similar ranges (Lillicrap et al., 2015, p. 4). Finally, the algorithm below shows the D-DPG algorithm.

Algorithm 9 D-DPG Algorithm, adapted from (Lillicrap et al., 2015, p. 5)

1: Randomly initialize critic network $Q(s, a|\theta^Q)$ and actor $\mu(s|\theta^\mu)$ with weights θ^Q and θ^μ.
2: Initialize target network Q' and μ' with weights $\theta^{Q'} \leftarrow \theta^Q$, $\theta^{\mu'} \leftarrow \theta^\mu$
3: Initialize replay buffer R
4: **for** $episode = 1, M$ **do**
5:    Initialize a random process $\mathcal{N}$ for action exploration   ▷ $\mathcal{N}$ may be any process that suits the environment.
6:    Receive initial observation state s_1
7:    **for** $t = 1, T$ **do**
8:        Select action $a_t = \mu(s_t|\theta^\mu) + \mathcal{N}_t$ according to the current policy and exploration noise
9:        Execute action a_t and observe reward r_t and observe new state s_{t+1}
10:        Store transition (s_t, a_t, r_t, s_{t+1}) in R

11:	Sample a random minibatch of N transitions (s_i, a_i, r_i, s_{i+1}) from R
12:	Set $y_i = r_i + \gamma Q'(s_{i+1}, \mu'(S_{i+1}|\theta^{\mu'})|\theta^{Q'})$
13:	Update critic by minimizing the loss: $L = \frac{1}{N}\sum_i (y_i - Q(s_i, a_i|\theta^Q))^2$
14:	Update the actor policy using the sampled policy gradient:

$$\nabla_\theta J(\mu_\theta) \approx \frac{1}{N}\sum_i \nabla_a Q(s, a|\theta^Q)|_{s=s_i, a=\mu(s_i)} \nabla_{\theta^\mu} \mu(s|\theta^\mu)|_{s_i}$$

15:	Update the target networks:	▷ Here $\tau \ll 1$

$$\theta^{Q'} \leftarrow \tau\theta^Q + (1-\tau)\theta^{Q'}$$

$$\theta^{\mu'} \leftarrow \tau\theta^\mu + (1-\tau)\theta^{\mu'}$$

16:	**end for**
17:	**end for**

The authors tested algorithm in the physics simulation environment MuJoCo (Todorov et al., 2012). There it solved over 20 tasks. Additionally, the authors tested their algorithm on the racing game *Torcs*, where it also performed well (see section 4.3).

4.2.4 Policy Iteration Using Monte Carlo Tree Search

Silver et al. (2017) developed a program, which they named AlphaGo Zero. While needing less training time, it was capable of outperforming all the previous versions: AlphaGo Fan (Silver et al., 2016), AlphaGo Lee[16] and AlphaGo Master[17].

For this, Silver et al. (2017) constructed a CNN f_θ with parameters θ, which takes the raw board representation s as input. The neural network then outputs some probability distribution p for taking certain actions and a scalar value v, which is the likelihood of the current player winning the game based on s. In other words, $f_\theta(s) = (p, v)$ (Silver et al., 2017, p. 354). The neural network is trained using a policy iteration procedure (see figure 2).

---

[16] See https://deepmind.com/research/alphago/alphago-korea/
[17] See https://deepmind.com/research/alphago/match-archive/master/

Silver et al. (2017) note that the Monte Carlo tree search (MCTS) can be viewed as a strong policy improvement procedure. Playing against previous versions of itself can be viewed as a strong policy evaluation operator (Silver et al., 2017, p. 354). The figure below illustrates the authors approach.

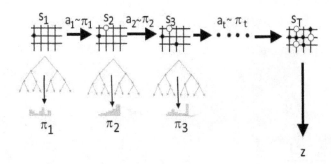

Figure 9: Self-Play Reinforcement Learning used in AlphaGo Zero, adapted from (Silver et al., 2017, p. 355)

During self-play, AlphaGo Zero executes a MCTS α_θ at every state s_t, which then outputs some search probabilities, such that $\pi_t = \alpha_\theta(s_t)$. Using this, the program selects an action $a_t \sim \pi_t$. The self-play continues until the game is over or some terminal state s_T is reached after which the winner z is determined (Silver et al., 2017, p. 355). Throughout the MCTS, the program simulates how the game will likely progress, using the current knowledge in the neural network as guidance as illustrated below.

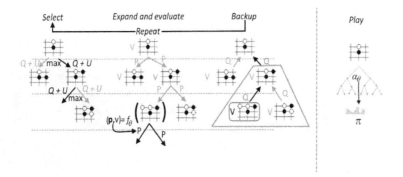

Figure 10: MCTS used in AlphaGo Zero, adapted from (Silver et al., 2017, p. 355)

Every edge in the search tree consists of the mean action value $Q(s, a)$, the total action value $W(s, a)$, a visit count $N(s, a)$ and the prior probability $P(s, a)$ for selecting that edge (Silver et al., 2017, p. 361). The MCTS consists of multiple steps, which are repeated several times: [18]

Step	Summary
Selection	Starting from the root s_0, the tree is traversed, selecting actions that return the highest values at every time step t, such that $a_t = \arg\max_a \left(Q(s, a) + U(s_t, a) \right)$, where $U(s_t, a) \propto \frac{P(s,a)}{1+N(s,a)}$ (Silver et al., 2016, p. 8) is the upper confidence bound. This step continues until some leaf node s' reached.
Evaluation and Expansion	The leaf node s' that the previous step reached will be evaluated by the neural network and the leaf node is expanded with new edges. The value v that was returned from the neural network will be backed up in the next step.

---

[18]Silver et al. (2017) used around 1600 simulations of MCTS before the search probabilities were returned. AlphaGo Zero required approximately $0.4s$ for each search.

| Backup | Every visited edge and node will be updated. The visit counter is incremented and the action value is adjusted to trace the mean of all the evaluations. |
| Play | At this point, the tree search is over and the agent has to select an action for the root state. The resulting search probabilities π are proportional to the visit count. |

Table 1: MCTS steps, adapted from (Silver et al., 2017, p. 355, 361)

These steps are returned until the game is over and a winner z is determined. Now, the neural network is adjusted to match its predictions v more closely to the actual winner z and the action probabilities p to the search probabilities. A gradient descent step is performed using the loss function

$$l = (z - v)^2 - \pi^T \log \boldsymbol{p} + c\|\theta\|^2, \tag{4.18}$$

where c is a parameter to prevent overfitting and was set to 10^{-4} (Silver et al., 2017, p. 355, 361). See section 4.3 for results.

4.2.5   Evolutionary Algorithms

Salimans et al. (2017) show that black box optimization algorithms, such as evolution strategies (Rechenberg and Eigen (1973) as cited in Salimans et al. (2017)), can be a viable alternative for solving RL tasks. They found evolution strategies (ES) to be a particularly parallelizable and robust technique for training neural network policies (Salimans et al., 2017, p. 1).

ES (Rechenberg and Eigen (1973) as cited in Salimans et al. (2017)) are closely inspired by evolution mechanisms in nature. Potential solutions are maintained as a population. At every iteration ("generation") the performance ("fitness") of the population is evaluated. The current population is then used to create the next generation of potential solutions (Salimans et al., 2017, p. 2).

For their work, Salimans et al. (2017) used natural evolution strategies (Wierstra et al., 2008, 2014). The goal of natural evolution strategies (NES) is to maximize the average objective function, i.e. fitness, $F(\theta)$, where θ are the parameters of the policy π_θ. The population is represented as a distribution over parameters $p_\psi(\theta)$, where the distribution is itself parameterized with ψ. In other words, the goal is to maximize $\mathbb{E}_{\theta \sim p_\psi} F(\theta)$ (Salimans et al., 2017, p. 2).

The population distribution is instantiated as an isotropic multivariate Gaussian distribution with mean ψ and fixed covariance $\sigma^2 I$ (Salimans et al., 2017, p. 2). This enabled the authors to rewrite the objective function to

$$\mathbb{E}_{\theta \sim p_\psi} F(\theta) = \mathbb{E}_{\epsilon \sim \mathcal{N}(0,I)} F(\theta + \sigma\epsilon). \tag{4.19}$$

Finally, by using stochastic gradient ascent, Salimans et al. (2017) optimize over θ with

$$\nabla_\theta \mathbb{E}_{\epsilon \sim \mathcal{N}(0,I)} F(\theta + \sigma\epsilon) = \frac{1}{\sigma} \mathbb{E}_{\epsilon \sim \mathcal{N}(0,I)} \Big(F(\theta + \sigma\epsilon)\epsilon \Big). \tag{4.20}$$

With sufficient samples, equation 4.20 can be estimated. The following algorithm shows this procedure.

Algorithm 10 Evolution Strategies, adapted from (Salimans et al., 2017, p. 3)

1: **Input:** Learning rate α, noise standard deviation σ, initial policy parameters θ_0
2: **for** $t = 0, 1, 2, \ldots$ **do**
3:     Sample $\epsilon_1, \ldots, \epsilon_n \sim \mathcal{N}(0, I)$
4:     Compute returns $F_i = F(\theta + \sigma\epsilon_i)$ for $i = 1, \ldots n$
5:     Set $\theta_{t+1} \leftarrow \theta_t + \alpha \frac{1}{n\sigma} \sum_{i=1}^{n} F_i \epsilon_i$
6: **end for**

Salimans et al. (2017) note the highly scalable nature of ES to multiple workers. Using known seeds for every worker, it is possible to reproduce the perturbation, i.e. the noise that was multiplied to the scalar reward. Hence, every worker only needs the scalar reward of episodes from other workers (Salimans et al., 2017, p. 3). A simple parallelized approach is shown in the next algorithm.

Algorithm 11 Parallelized ES, adapted from (Salimans et al., 2017, p. 3)

1: **Input:** Learning rate α, noise standard deviation σ, initial policy parameters θ_0
2: **Initialize:** n workers with known seeds, and initial parameters θ_0
3: **for** $t = 0, 1, 2, \ldots$ **do**
4:     **for** each worker $i = 1, \ldots, n$ **do**
5:         Sample $\epsilon_i \sim \mathcal{N}(0, I)$
6:         Compute returns $F_i = F(\theta_t + \sigma \epsilon_i)$
7:     **end for**
8:     Send all scalar returns F_i from each worker to every other worker
9:     **for** each worker $i = 1, \ldots, n$ **do**
10:         Reconstruct all perturbations ϵ_j for $j = 1, \ldots, n$ using known random seeds
11:         Set $\theta_{t+1} \leftarrow \theta_t + \alpha \frac{1}{n\sigma} \sum_{j=1}^{n} F_j \epsilon_j$
12:     **end for**
13: **end for**

To ensure the exploration of many actions, Salimans et al. (2017) use virtual batch normalization (Ioffe and Szegedy, 2015; Salimans et al., 2016). However, this requires additional forward passes in the network, which is computationally more expensive. The authors note, that without virtual batch normalization, ES performed poorly in their experiments (Salimans et al., 2017, p. 1).

In the end, using a total of 80 machines with 1440 CPU cores, ES was able to solve 3D humanoid walking task in just 10 minutes. Furthermore, it also performed well on Atari 2600 games (see section 4.3) it was better on 23 games and worse on 28 when compared to A3C (Mnih et al., 2016).

Deep Genetic Algorithm

Although ES (Salimans et al., 2017) do not directly compute the gradients but rather approximate them using many samples, they can still be seen as a gradient-based approach. Furthermore, ES managed to ignite the interest of using evolutionary algorithms in the RL domain.

Petroski Such et al. (2017) investigated how completely gradient-free methods could work in a RL environment, specifically focusing on genetic algorithms (Holland, 1992). Genetic algorithms (GA) are also very closely related to natural evolution. Similarly to the previous section, a population $\mathcal{P}$ with $\mathcal{N}$ individuals is tested for their performance. Petroski Such et al. (2017) use the best performing individuals, which are in fact a parameter vector θ of a neural network, to *breed* the next generation. Much like in nature, the offspring is mutated by blurring the parameter vector with Gaussian noise. Also, Petroski Such et al. (2017) utilize the *elitism* technique, keeping the best individual unchanged from the previous generation. This algorithm is depicted below.

Algorithm 12 Simple Genetic Algorithm, adapted from (Petroski Such et al., 2017, p. 3)

1: **Input:** Mutation power σ, population size N, number of selected individuals T, policy initialization routine ϕ
2: **for** $g = 1, 2, \ldots G$ generations **do**
3:     **for** $i = 1, 2, \ldots N$ in next generation's population **do**
4:         **if** g=1 **then**
5:             $\mathcal{P}_i^g = \phi\big(\mathcal{N}(0, I)\big)$ ▷ initialize random deep neural network
6:             $F_i^g = F(\mathcal{P}_i^g)$ ▷ assess its fitness
7:         **else**
8:             **if** $i = 1$ **then**
9:                 $\mathcal{P}_i^g = \mathcal{P}_i^{g-1}$
10:                $F_i^g = F_i g - 1$ ▷ copy the elite
11:             **else**
12:                 $k = \text{uniformRandom}(1, T)$ ▷ select parent
13:                 Sample $\epsilon \sim \mathcal{N}(0, I)$
14:                 $\mathcal{P}_i^g = \mathcal{P}_k^{g-1} + \sigma\epsilon$ ▷ mutate parent
15:                 $F_i^g = F(\mathcal{P}_i^g)$ ▷ assess its fitness
16:             **end if**
17:         **end if**
18:     **end for**
19:     Sort $\mathcal{P}^g$ and F^g with descending oder by F^g
20: **end for**
21: **Return:** highest performing policy $\mathcal{P}_1^g$

Furthermore, Petroski Such et al. (2017) note that training performance of deep neural networks can be increased by using available algorithms from the neuroevolution domain.

One of those is novelty search (Lehman and Stanley, 2011), which chooses the offspring such that the offspring's behavior characteristics $(\text{BC}(\pi))$ are as *novel* as possible compared to other individuals; more specifically, the average distance to the closest k BC, calculated by a behavior distance function. Also, some individual's BC are stored in an archive with some probability (Petroski Such et al., 2017, p. 3-4). This algorithm is shown below.

Algorithm 13 Novelty Search, adapted from (Petroski Such et al., 2017, p. 15)

1: **Input:** Mutation power σ, population size N, number of selected individuals to reproduce T, policy initialization routine ϕ, empty archive $\mathcal{A}$, archive insertion probability p
2: **for** $g = 1, 2, \ldots G$ generations **do**
3:      **for** $i = 1, 2, \ldots N$ in next generation's population **do**
4:          **if** $g = 1$ **then**
5:             $\mathcal{P}_i^g = \phi\left(\mathcal{N}(0, I)\right)$ ▷ initialize random deep neural network
6:             $BC_i^g = BC(\mathcal{P}_i^g); \; F_i^g = F(\mathcal{P}_i^g)$
7:          **else**
8:             **if** $i = 1$ **then**
9:                 $\mathcal{P}_i^g = \mathcal{P}_i^{g-1}; \; F_i^g = F_i^{g-1}$
10:                 $BC_i^g = BC_i^{g-1}$
11:             **else**
12:                 $k = \text{uniformRandom}(1, T)$ ▷ select parent
13:                 Sample $\epsilon \sim \mathcal{N}(0, I)$
14:                 $\mathcal{P}_i^g = \mathcal{P}_k^{g-1} + \sigma\epsilon$ ▷ mutate parent
15:                 $F_i^g = F(\mathcal{P}_i^g)$
16:             **end if**
17:          **end if**
18:      **end for**
19:      **for** $i = 1, 2, \ldots N$ in next generation population **do**
20:          $\mathcal{N}_i^g = dist(BC_i^g, \mathcal{A} \cup BC^g)$
21:          Insert BC_i^g into $\mathcal{A}$ with probability p
22:      **end for**
23:      Sort $(\mathcal{P}^g, BC^g, F^g)$ with descending oder by $\mathcal{N}^g$
24: **end for**
25: **Return:** highest performing policy

The authors tested their algorithms on some of the games in the Atari 2600 environment and compared their results with those from other algorithms. More specifically, these were

- DQN (section 4.1.1)

- ES (section 4.2.5)

- A3C (section 4.2.1)

- Random Search

They found deep-GA to be competitive with the other algorithms (see section 4.3).

4.3 Performance of the Algorithms

The two main testbeds for RL benchmarks are the Atari 2600 testbed (Bellemare et al., 2012) and the physics simulation MuJoCo (Todorov et al., 2012). The results on these testbeds will be shown in this order in the next section. The final part will be dedicated to various other performance measures.

4.3.1 Atari 2600

Value-Based Approaches and A3C

To asses the performance of their Rainbow agent, Hessel et al. (2017) compared their performance with several other learning agents. They test their algorithm against all the value-based approaches that were presented in this chapter, A3C and also noisy DQN (Fortunato et al., 2017). When Hessel et al. (2017) compared their Rainbow agent to the other baselines, they found their agent to be **significantly** better.

Table 2 shows the agents' scores on the Atari 2600 testbed. These show the median normalized scores such that 0% is random behavior and 100% corresponds to the average human score. In other words, scores above 100% indicate super-human performance. Furthermore, the agent's performance is evaluated using two testing regimes: *no-ops* and *human starts*.

For the *no-ops* testing regime, a random number of no-op[19] actions are performed at the beginning of each episode whereas in the *human-starts* testing regime, the agent started at a random point from a human player's trajectory (Nair et al., 2015, p. 6).

---

[19]No-op actions are actions in which the agent does nothing. *Passing*, in other words.

Agent	no-ops	human starts
DQN	79%	68%
DDQN (*)	117%	110%
Prioritized DDQN (*)	140%	128%
Dueling DDQN (*)	151%	117%
A3C (*)	-	116%
Noisy DQN	118%	102%
Distributional DQN	164%	125%
Rainbow	223%	153%

Table 2: Median normalized scores. Scores from agents marked with an asterisk stem from their respective paper. DQN's scores are from Wang et al. (2015). The remaining scores are from Hessel et al. (2017) (their own implementations). Table adapted from (Hessel et al., 2017, p. 5)

Another major advantage for Rainbow over the other agents is the learning time. Hessel et al. (2017) ran each agent on a single graphical processing unit (GPU). Rainbow achieved DQN's final performance after $7M$ frames, which is less than 10 hours of wall-clock time (Hessel et al., 2017, p. 5). After around $44M$ frames, Rainbow already performed better than the final performance of the distributional DQN, which was the state-of-the-art at that time.

Since the Rainbow agent is a compilation of several algorithms, Hessel et al. (2017) investigated, which contribution to Rainbow was the most important. In other words, removing which part let to the greatest decrease in performance. The order of importance for the Rainbow agent is (Hessel et al., 2017, p. 6):

1. Prioritized Replay (substantial loss)

2. Multi-Step Learning (substantial loss)

3. Distributional Learning (significant loss, but slightly less than 1. or 2.)

4. Noisy Nets (slight loss)

5. Dueling Network (barely noticeable)

6. Double Q-Learning (barely noticeable)

For a more detailed view on the individual games, the supplementary material from Hessel et al. (2017) is referred to.

Trust Region Policy Optimization

Schulman et al. (2015) tested their TRPO algorithms only on 7 Atari 2600 games. They compared TRPO to random behavior, expert human play, DQN and UCC-I, an algorithm based on MCTS (Guo et al., 2014).

Agent	Mean score
Random	111.54
Human (Mnih et al., 2013)	8350, 29
DQN (Mnih et al., 2013)	1284.0
UCC-I (Guo et al., 2014)	4365.14
TRPO - single path	920.13
TRPO - vine	1473.79

Table 3: Mean scores on 7 Atari 2600 games. The sum of the scores was calculated and divided by 7. Table based on (Schulman et al., 2015, p. 8)

It must be noted however, that the TRPO algorithm was not specifically designed for the Atari 2600 games, unlike the other algorithms it was tested against. This test was only conducted to show the generality of TRPO, whose real strength lies in the MuJoCo tests.

Evolutionary Algorithms

To compare the performance of evolutionary algorithms and other algorithms, the data from Petroski Such et al. (2017) will be used. Here, Petroski Such et al. (2017) compared their simple GA algorithm on 13 Atari 2600 games against ES (Salimans et al., 2017), DQN (Mnih et al., 2013, 2015), random search and A3C (Mnih et al., 2016). Petroski Such et al. (2017) chose not to compare their algorithm against the Rainbow agent (Hessel et al., 2017) since the GA algorithm does not incorporate any other features and is thus, a *vanilla* version. As such, a fair comparison is to benchmark it against the vanilla DQN version (Petroski Such et al., 2017, p. 5). The authors note the difficulty of comparing the algorithms as its mostly apples-to-oranges comparisons (Petroski Such et al., 2017, p. 4).

	DQN	ES	RS	GA	GA	A3C
Frames, Time	$200M, \sim 7-10d$	$1B, \sim 1h$	$1B, \sim 1h$	$1B, \sim 1h$	$4B, \sim 4h$	$1.28B, \sim 4d$
Forward Passes	$450M$	$250M$	$250M$	$250M$	$1B$	$960M$
Backward Passes	$400M$	0	0	0	0	$640M$
Operations	$1.25B$ U	$250M$ U	$250M$ U	$250M$ U	$1B$ U	$2.24B$ U
Amidar	**978**	112	151	216	294	264
Assault	4.280	1.674	642	819	1.006	**5.475**
Asterix	4.359	1.440	1.175	1.885	2.392	**22.140**
Asteroids	1.365	1.562	1.404	2.056	2.056	**4.475**
Atlantis	279.987	**1.267.410**	45.257	79.793	125.883	911.091
Enduro	**729**	95	32	39	50	-82
Frostbite	797	370	1.379	**4.801**	5.623	191
Gravitar	473	**805**	290	462	637	304
Kangoroo	7.259	**11.200**	1.773	8.667	10.920	94
Seaquest	**5.861**	1.390	559	807	1.241	2.355
Skiing	-13.062	-15.442	-8.816	**-6.995**	**-6.522**	-10.911
Venture	163	760	547	**810**	**1.093**	23
Zaxxon	5.363	6.380	2.943	5.183	6.827	**24.622**

Table 4: Evolutionary algorithm scores on 13 Atari 2600 games. Table based on (Petroski Such et al., 2017, p. 6)

Salimans et al. (2017) did a more extensive test on their ES against A3C (Mnih et al., 2016). In their test, they found that out of 51 Atari 2600 games, their one-hour[20] ES

---

[20]Their one-hour ES required about as much computations as the one-day A3C (Salimans et al., 2017, p. 2).

outperformed A3C in 23 games and performed worse on 28 (Salimans et al., 2017, p. 2).

4.3.2 MuJuCo

Trust Region Policy Optimization

Schulman et al. (2015) tested their TRPO algorithm on three simulated robots in the MuJoCo simulation environment. These were: swimmer, walker and hopper. Schulman et al. (2015) compared TRPO (vine and single path procedure) to a cross-entropy method (Szita and Lörincz, 2006), covariance-matrix adaptation (Hansen and Ostermeier, 1996), a natural gradient method (Kakade, 2002), empirical Fisher information matrix and max KL (see Schulman et al. (2015) for additional information). The TRPO algorithm outperformed all the other methods and solved the problems with good solutions (Schulman et al., 2015, p. 7).

Evolutionary Algorithms

Salimans et al. (2017) used their ES algorithm to train the same policy architecture as in TRPO (Schulman et al., 2015). They managed to reach TRPO's final performance after interacting with the simulated environment for 5 million timesteps (Salimans et al., 2017, p. 7).

Furthermore, Salimans et al. (2017) demonstrated the scalability of ES when they distributed ES across 80 machines and 1.440 CPU cores and solved the 3D humanoid locomotion task in just 10 minutes (Salimans et al., 2017, p. 7-8).

Petroski Such et al. (2017) also evaluated their GA algorithm on the 3D humanoid task and managed to reach the performance of ES. However, their algorithm required far more computations. The reason for this increased necessity for computation is still unclear (Petroski Such et al., 2017, p. 7-8).

Deep Deterministic Policy Gradient

Lillicrap et al. (2015) tested their algorithm on over 20 different settings in the MuJoCo environment. For both low-dimensional (positions and angles of the simulated entity) and high-dimensional state descriptions (pixels from the screen; downscaled), their algorithm performed overall very well. In fact, in some cases it outperformed a planning algorithm, which has complete access to the simulated world (Lillicrap et al., 2015, p. 1,4-7, 11-14).

When Lillicrap et al. (2015) experimented with their algorithm's configurations, they either removed the target network or the batch normalization. For the best performance, both of these components were required. This especially applies to target networks, where the removal lead to a significant decrease in performance in many environments (Lillicrap et al., 2015, p. 5).

Asynchronous Actor Critic Method
Mnih et al. (2016) tested only their A3C algorithm in the MuJoCo environment in 14 tasks. Overall, their algorithm found good solutions to these tasks in relatively short time (p. 7, supplementary material of Mnih et al. (2016)).

4.3.3 Various Measures

Go
Arguably, one of the greatest achievements in the field of AI in general was done by Silver et al. (2017) when researchers in Google's DeepMind defeated humans in Go.

AlphaGo Fan (Silver et al., 2016), an earlier version of AlphaGo Zero (Silver et al., 2017), was tested against several other Go programs, where AlphaGo Fan had a win rate of 99.8%. Later, it was tested against Fan Hui and defeated him 5 - 0 (Silver et al., 2016, p. 1). A later version, AlphaGo Lee, played against the world champion Lee Sedol, who was defeated 4 - 1[21].

Currently, AlphaGo Zero (Silver et al., 2017) is one of the most recent versions. Its Elo rating stands at around 5185 (Silver et al., 2017, p. 358), making it very likely one of the strongest, if not the strongest, Go-playing entity in the world.

Torcs
Both asynchronous methods (Mnih et al., 2016) and deep deterministic policy gradient methods (Lillicrap et al., 2015) were tested on the driving emulator TORCS, which has more realistic graphics compared to Atari 2600 games.

---

[21]See http://www.alphago-games.com/#leesedol - Accessed on 23.3.2018

The best run from (Lillicrap et al., 2015) (from pixel inputs) had a score of around 1876 (detailed test settings were not available, see (Lillicrap et al., 2015, 7)). For asynchronous methods (Mnih et al., 2016), the A3C algorithm performed the best out of all the asynchronous methods at every testing configuration, consistently scoring above 3000 in every setting (p. 5, supplementary material of Mnih et al. (2016)).

Image Hard Maze

In this test, Petroski Such et al. (2017) compared their GA against several other algorithms in a image maze test. This environment is shown in figure 11.

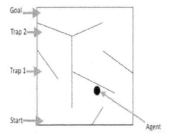

Figure 11: Image Hard Maze, reprinted and adapted from (Petroski Such et al., 2017, p. 8)

Here, the agent, which fully observes the environment, has to navigate through the maze while avoiding multiple traps (local optima). Petroski Such et al. (2017) found that reward-driven algorithms got stuck in the traps, while their novelty search GA managed to solve the maze and find the exit (Petroski Such et al., 2017, p. 8-9).

5 Discussion

In this chapter, several shortcomings in the field of DRL that were identified in this research will be discussed. Furthermore, new research direction will be proposed. In some cases, the findings and structure of this chapter overlap with Arulkumaran et al. (2017) and Li (2017) due to the similarity in the topics (see section 2).

5.1 Exploration vs. Exploitation

The exploration vs. exploitation dilemma is a fundamental problem ever since the very beginning of RL and is best illustrated by a simple example.

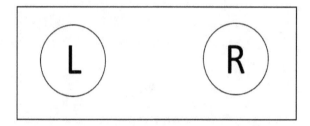

Figure 12: Exploration vs. Exploitation Example (by author)

Figure 12 shows two buttons, where either button can be pressed by the agent at every timestep and each button press immediately rewards the agent. After some timesteps (e.g. 100), the agent noticed that the left button seems to give positive rewards (+1) while the right button gives negative rewards (−1), even after several continuous presses of the right button (e.g. 20). Hence, the agent concludes that the optimal policy is to press the left button.

The agent could, however, press the right button for 100 times consecutively and be rewarded with +500, which is a superior policy than before. Similarly, continuously pressing the left button could eventually give the agent a reward of −500, nullifying all its previous work.

This example seems very trivial but it shows the underlying problem in RL: what is the ideal trade-off between exploration and exploitation. Because this is a well-known problem, extensive work has already been done (see Thrun (1992)). There have been several approaches to this problem in the results from chapter 4. For example, DQN uses ϵ-greedy exploration (Mnih et al., 2015, p. 535), novelty-search GA selects the offspring based on how novel their behavior is (Petroski Such et al., 2017, p. 4) and AlphaGo Zero uses an upper-confidence bound to give weights to unexplored actions (Silver et al., 2017, p. 355).

Recent research includes robotic agents that use demonstrations to address the exploration problem, which can be used on multi-step tasks with very sparse reward signals (Nair et al., 2017); count-based exploration, where uncertainty is measured by density models, which are then used to determine a pseudo-count measure for exploration (Bellemare et al., 2016) (further discussed by Tang et al. (2017)); exploration strategies based on previously acquired knowledge (Gupta et al., 2018); curiosity-driven exploration strategies, which is based on the information gain to the agent's belief about the environment's dynamics, i.e. the agent is more motivated to take actions that deliver the greatest gain (biggest update) to the agent's belief (Houthooft et al., 2016); exploration based on under-appreciated rewards (Nachum et al., 2016).

The exploration vs. exploitation dilemma remains an open research question, due to its massive complexity. The research mentioned above show however compelling research directions.

5.2 Need for Rewards

Almost all of the algorithms presented in section 4 have the underlying assumption of a given reward function. The reward structure is heavily dependent on the task at hand. It can either be a positive reward only once the task has successfully been performed or it can have a *dynamic* form. An example for the first case would be in the game of chess, where winning the game would give the agent a reward of $+1$ or -1 otherwise. The latter one is known as reward shaping. Here, the agent gets increasing rewards the closer it gets to the goal (Brys et al., 2015, p. 3353).

Both these paradigms have each their strengths and weaknesses and their usage depends on what problem the agent is trying to solve. Shaped rewards in the game of chess, for example, could turn out to be problematic. Surely, capturing the opponent's queen is generally very helpful, but if it costs the player the game then it was not a good option. The agent could learn that capturing the queen gives a very high reward and could thus base its entire game plan on capturing the queen and not actually on winning the game. Sparse rewards encourage the agent to focus on the final goal, but are very hard to learn from. If the task is too complex and rewards are too sparse, then the agent would just wander around in its environment without ever learning anything.

It seems that reward engineering is an intricate and complex task and one could ask if there is a way of extracting the reward structure from the task itself. This is also known as inverse reinforcement learning (IRL) (Ng et al., 2000).

Learning by shaped rewards is generally easier, because it is easier to learn if the agent knows what effect his actions have. It would be interesting to see some implementations in conjunction with natural language processing. If an agent is given a goal via text input, then the reward function should shift accordingly to match the goal.

5.3 Knowledge Reusability

Most of the time when a RL agent is trained on a particular task it can only stay in that domain. Although its algorithm may stay the same throughout multiple tasks, when it changes its task, the policy must also be retrained from anew, even if the tasks were rather similar.

Ideally, the agent should be trained on a task and perform reasonably well on similar tasks. This is especially important in robotics. Training a robot in the real physical world is expensive, both in time and financial costs. It is much more practical to train the agent in a simulated environment and then have the agent perform similar tasks in the real world.

Training an agent in a simulated environment and then have it perform in the real world has recently been explored by Zhu et al. (2016). Here, an agent interacted with a simulated room, which contained multiple furnitures. The agent could move freely and received visual observations as input. The goal of the agent was to navigate to a particular target (e.g. to the book shelf that is somewhere in the room). After being trained in the simulated environment, the agent was then (after some minor adjustments) deployed in the real world, where it used the previously learning knowledge from the simulations to navigate to the specified targets.

Depending on the task the agent is supposed to solve, training can take a long time (see section 5.4). In the domain of games, it would be interesting to see if an agent trained on one game of Pong was able to play a *similar* game of Pong without any adjustments, thus saving most of the training time on the second game. This approach would fall into the category of model-based RL. One could imagine a neural network that extracts the features of the input and stores that as a state in the agent's memory. When played on another game, the neural network may recognize the similar features of that other input and after minimal automatic adjustments to itself proceed to play the other game effectively.

5.4 Inefficiency

When viewing the performance of the Rainbow agent (Hessel et al., 2017) it can be seen that after approximately $200M$ frames the peak performance is achieved. The Rainbow agent surpassed the median human performance at around $20M$ frames. Considering the fact that one frame lasts for $\frac{1}{60}s$, then the training time until average human performance was reached was

$$\left((20.000.000 \cdot \frac{1}{60})/60\right)/60 = 92.\overline{592} \approx 92.6h.$$

In other words, it took the Rainbow agent around 92.6 hours until it reached median human performance. This is a sobering number, considering the fact that most humans pick up game mechanics after only a few seconds of exposure. Of course, most games are made *by* humans *for* humans. Furthermore, humans come *built-in* with notions of cause and effect and action and reaction and had millions of years to evolve up to this state. It seems hardly to be a fair comparison, however, in this technological age, time is of the essence, which is important, for example, in domains like financial transactions. For RL agents to be used in every day real world applications, they need not necessarily have to have super-human performance as long as they are around as good as humans. However, no human would need $92.6h$ for understanding the game mechanics of Atari games.

This is not a phenomenon solely restricted to the Rainbow agent. In model-free methods, such as Rainbow, most of the valuable information is not used, leading the agent to require more and more samples.

One of the possibilities for higher sample efficiency lies in model-based approaches, which will be discussed in section 5.6.

5.5 Multi-Agent Reinforcement Learning

Most of the research covered in section 4 was concerned about single-agent RL. If there was some other moving entity in the environment, then, in the single-agent case, it would just be registered as part of the environment. There is, however, the possibility of multiple agents working together to reach a common goal. This domain is called multi-agent reinforcement learning (Busoniu et al., 2008). Multi-agent reinforcement learning (MARL) is can find application in robotics, distributional control, telecommunication and economics (Busoniu et al., 2008, p. 156).

The central issue in MARL is the formal statement of the multi-agent learning goal. Because the agent's returns are strongly correlated, they cannot be maximized independently (Busoniu et al., 2008, p. 160). To address this issue, the literature several approaches have been presented. Generally, these approaches can be divided in the following two directions, which target either the

- stability of the agent's learning dynamics or

- adaptation to the changing behavior of the agents (Busoniu et al., 2008, p. 156).

Another problem in the MARL setting is the curse of dimensionality, which is more severe than in the single-agent case. Here, the complexity is also exponential to the number of agents (Busoniu et al., 2008, p. 160).

Recently, Foerster et al. (2017) have attempted to combine experience replay in the multi-agent setting to increase the learning stability. They addressed a problem that occurred with independent Q-learning (IQL) (Tan, 1993). In IQL, each agent learns their own policy independently from other agents and view those as part of the environment. Because of this, as mentioned by Foerster et al. (2017), the environment becomes nonstationary, which makes it difficult to apply experience replay. This is due to the fact that the dynamics responsible for generating the data in the agent's memory does not correspond to the current dynamics (Foerster et al., 2017, p. 3-5).

The authors proposed the following methods to make the multi-agent setting compatible with experience replay:

1. "using a multi-agent variant of importance sampling to naturally decay obsolete data and

2. conditioning each agent's value function on a *fingerprint* that disambiguates the age of the data sampled from the replay memory." (Foerster et al., 2017, p. 1)

Another important aspect in MARL is the communication between agents. This was recently investigated by Foerster et al. (2016). Here, the authors used advancements in deep learning to enable effective information sharing between the agents.

One of the most interesting fields for MARL is the testing in MOBA games (do Nascimento Silva and Chaimowicz, 2017b), which has recently drawn much attention, when Dendi[22] was beaten by OpenAI's Dota 2 bot (OpenAI, n.d.). Although there have been previous attempts at MOBA games (do Nascimento Silva and Chaimowicz, 2017a; Wilich, 2015), the fully cooperative setting of MOBA games has yet to be solved.

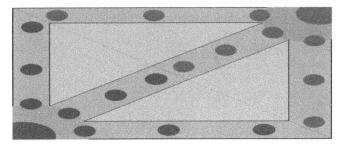

Figure 13: Multiplayer Online Battle Arena; General outline of a typical map in MOBA games, adapted from (do Nascimento Silva and Chaimowicz, 2017b, p. 2)

---

[22]Danil "**Dendi**" Ishutin is currently considered to be one of the best professional Dota 2 players.

In MOBA games the player typically controls only one unit known as a *hero* or occasionally *champion*. These have their individual health and magic points, whose value can vary slightly depending on the hero's archetype (e.g. *strength* class heroes have high health but only very little magic points). Normally, these heroes have some special abilities, which cost magic points to execute. The effects from those abilities are different for every hero; they can heal, inflict damage, teleport units, revive units, spawn temporary units and so on. Aside from heroes, non-playable, computer controlled units, which are known as *creeps*, always follow a linear pattern and march towards the enemy base. The goal is to destroy the other team's towers and finally their base (see figure 13). For more details on the MOBA game mechanics, do Nascimento Silva and Chaimowicz (2017b) are referred to.

Most of the popular MOBA games such as *League of Legens, Dota 2, Heroes of Newerth* and *Smite* are played in a five-versus-five player setting. In other words, two teams consisting of five heroes play against each other and try to conquer the other team's base. So far, only the one-versus-one setting in Dota 2 was partially solved (some restrictions regarding hero choice and *item build*) by researchers from the OpenAI team.

Clearly, the next goal is to attempt a multiplayer setting in MOBA games, such as a two-versus-two *laning phase*. What makes this especially appealing for research in RL is the fact that agents must have some strategy, precise control over their unit(s) and execute various kinds of decision making (e.g. when to chase other heroes, when to engage, when to retreat and so on) and the fact that MOBA games are only *partially observable*, meaning the agent has no complete information about the environment[23], which is a more realistic assumption about most problems. The most interesting aspect would be seeing how agents cooperate, save each other and even coordinate their abilities to defeat the opponent's heroes.

Since most heroes have their individual roles, perhaps revisiting and extending some ideas from Wilson et al. (2008) to the domain of MOBA games could yield some success.

---

[23]Most MOBA games have what is commonly known as *fog of war*. These are parts of the map that are covered in dark shadow and are only revealed when allied units walk into those areas. Opponents may be hiding in that fog and potentially ambush the player. Since those areas are not visible, the agent does not have complete information about the current state, hence making it only *partially observable*.

5.6 Model-Based Reinforcement Learning

All of the research covered in section 4 was based on either value-based or policy-based approaches. These are so called *model-free* methods. There is, however, another way of solving RL problems, which is the model-based approach, where the agent learns a model of the environment.

Although model-based methods can be more sample efficient, their peak performance does not match model-free methods (Nagabandi et al., 2017, p. 1). Because of the greater sample efficiency, model-based methods can be more appealing in real world applications such as robotics. Training robots in a model-free fashion would yield higher performance but the amount of data and training time required would make it too impractical. Model-based methods, on the other hand, learn based on their model, thus requiring much less interactions with the actual environment.

	Model-Free	Model-Based
Pros	high peak performance	very sample efficient
Cons	requires many samples	medium peak performance

Table 5: Short summary of the model-based vs. model-free comparison

Viewing table 5 it is natural to want to combine each of the approaches' strengths as they appear to be complementary. And indeed, there seems to be indications that even the human brain may in fact be working as a both *model-based and model-free* learner (Gläscher et al., 2010, p. 585). Combining model-based and model-free methods has recently been explored by Nagabandi et al. (2017).

5.7 Proposed Research Directions

Given all the information so far, the question emerges, which next goals should be pursued. One such goals is the reusability of knowledge, where games can be used as a testbed. First attempts have been made (Asawa et al., 2017; Braylan et al., 2015) but more research is required. Potential targets here could be the game series *Tekken* or *Super Smash Bros.* Most of the games in *Tekken* have very similar dynamics and control. If a player is good in one game, then there is a very high chance that the same player will perform in newer games significantly better than a completely new player. Ideally, the RL agent should perform similarly. The same goes for the *Super Smash. Bros.* game series, although this game could arguably be more difficult due to more dynamic gameplay.

However, here, some domain knowledge is already known beforehand. It is known that, for example, *Tekken 2* is very closely related in game dynamics to *Tekken 3*. The difficulty lies in the greater state, action and input dimensions. The goal here is also in saving training time. After being trained on *Tekken 2* for several hours until reasonable performance is achieved, then the agent should perform also reasonably well in *Tekken 3* within minutes, without explicitly telling the agent about the games' similarities.

In terms of board games, another interesting game would be *Stratego*.

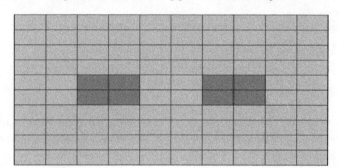

Figure 14: Stratego game field, (by author): each player can put their pieces freely on the green squares. The blue squares cannot be visited.

First attempts at the game of Stratego have already been made (Arts, 2010; Smith, 2015) but more research is needed. Stratego has some interesting aspects that are not available in other board games. For instance, the environment is only partially observable. This is because the enemies' units are hidden from the agent, until they are attacked. Not only does the agent not know the strength of those units, it also has to *remember* already attacked units, since they are revealed in the turn they were attacked. If the attacked unit survived, its value is concealed from the agent in the next turn.

In terms of game complexity, the state-space is around 10^{115} and the game-tree complexity is around 10^{535} (compared to 10^{172} and 10^{360} respectively for the game of Go) (Arts, 2010, p. 11).

For MARL settings, future work includes, as already mentioned, the n-versus-n settings in MOBA games, where $n > 1$. Other interesting targets for this field (and many other domains) could potentially be *Minecraft*, where certain sub-tasks (e.g. navigation) have already been investigated (Oh et al., 2016; Tessler et al., 2016). Here, the state-space is so enormously big that for RL purposes it might as well just be infinite. Potential targets here could lie in construction, where one (or multiple) agents have to reconstruct a certain structure when given a *target image*. But more general problems can be studied too. How could an agent survive in Minecraft? How should it behave against other agents when competing for resources? There are many possibilities, making Minecraft an interesting target for future RL research. *Project Malmo* (Johnson et al., 2016) has been established by researchers from Microsoft to facilitate research using Minecraft.

6 Conclusion

This thesis showed some of the recent research conducted in DRL. Generally, this research can be divided into value-based, policy-based or model-based RL, although the latter one did have see much attention in terms of research activity. The first two categories have shown great success in domains like Atari games and control in physics simulations. The following table 6 shows a short overview of the topics that were covered in this thesis.

Value-Based	Policy-Based
DQN	A3C
Double DQN	TRPO
Prioritized Replay	D-DPG
Dueling Network	Policy Iteration with MCTS
Distributional RL	Evolutionary Algorithms
Rainbow	

Table 6: Short overview of the covered research

At this point, it is important to take a step back and view the entirety of AI in general. There seems to be a general division of AI stages: artificial narrow, general and super-intelligence[24]. Artificial narrow intelligence include those systems that are designed to serve a singular purpose, whereas artificial general intelligence is able to tackle multiple varying tasks, just like a human is able to learn and adapt to new environments. Designing an AI system for every single task is very tedious. Ideally, one would want to have just one system for every problem. As of now, RL is the closest *thing* we humans have to artificial general intelligence, which makes it, naturally, a very compelling target for research.

Furthermore, there seems to a recurring theme in the domain of machine learning in general, i.e. a lot of achievements were derived from nature. Some examples of this include RL itself, which is based on the *Law of Effect* (Thorndike, 1927), neural networks, which

---

[24]Artificial super intelligence would be able to solve any problem in any domain much better than any human.

are based on the structure of the brain and genetic algorithms, which are based on the notion of *survival of the fittest*. It makes sense to attempt the same in RL. Because the human brain seems to show indications of working as a both model-based and model-free learner (Gläscher et al., 2010, p. 585), the combination of these two paradigms will likely show great success as well.

There are still many open research questions. How can the multiagent setting in MOBA games be solved? How can a learned policy be reused for other tasks? What could be possible solutions to fundamental problems such as exploration vs. exploitation or the design of reward functions? These questions have yet to be answered.

Fortunately, organizations such as OpenAI, which associated with the prominent figure *Elon Musk*, are attempting to solve the multiagent MOBA problem for the popular game *Dota 2*. These positive associations will hopefully take RL out to the public, sparking more interest for the field and maybe accelerate the research pace.

References

A. Arts. Competitive Play in Stratego, Master Thesis, 2010.

K. Arulkumaran, M. P. Deisenroth, M. Brundage, and A. A. Bharath. A Brief Survey of Deep Reinforcement Learning. *IEEE Signal Processing Magazine*, 2017.

C. Asawa, C. Elamri, and D. Pan. Using Transfer Learning Between Games to Improve Deep Reinforcement Learning Performance and Stability. *Stanford University*, 2017.

M. G. Bellemare, Y. Naddaf, J. Veness, and M. Bowling. The Arcade Learning Environment: An Evaluation Platform for General Agents. *ArXiv e-prints*, July 2012.

M. G. Bellemare, S. Srinivasan, G. Ostrovski, T. Schaul, D. Saxton, and R. Munos. Unifying Count-Based Exploration and Intrinsic Motivation. *ArXiv e-prints*, June 2016.

M. G. Bellemare, W. Dabney, and R. Munos. A Distributional Perspective on Reinforcement Learning. *ArXiv e-prints*, July 2017.

A. Braylan, M. Hollenbeck, E. Meyerson, and R. Miikkulainen. Reuse of Neural Modules for General Video Game Playing. *ArXiv e-prints*, Dec. 2015.

T. Brys, A. Harutyunyan, H. B. Suay, S. Chernova, M. E. Taylor, and A. Nowé. Reinforcement Learning from Demonstration through Shaping. In *IJCAI*, 2015.

L. Busoniu, R. Babuska, and B. De Schutter. A comprehensive survey of multiagent reinforcement learning. *IEEE Trans. Systems, Man, and Cybernetics, Part C*, 2008.

V. do Nascimento Silva and L. Chaimowicz. On the Development of Intelligent Agents for MOBA Games. *ArXiv e-prints*, June 2017a.

V. do Nascimento Silva and L. Chaimowicz. MOBA: a New Arena for Game AI. *ArXiv e-prints*, 2017b.

J. Foerster, N. Nardelli, G. Farquhar, T. Afouras, P. H. S. Torr, P. Kohli, and S. Whiteson. Stabilising Experience Replay for Deep Multi-Agent Reinforcement Learning. *ArXiv e-prints*, Feb. 2017.

J. N. Foerster, Y. M. Assael, N. de Freitas, and S. Whiteson. Learning to Communicate with Deep Multi-Agent Reinforcement Learning. *ArXiv e-prints*, May 2016.

M. Fortunato, M. Gheshlaghi Azar, B. Piot, J. Menick, I. Osband, A. Graves, V. Mnih, R. Munos, D. Hassabis, O. Pietquin, C. Blundell, and S. Legg. Noisy Networks for Exploration. *ArXiv e-prints*, June 2017.

J. Gläscher, N. Daw, P. Dayan, and J. P. O'Doherty. States versus rewards: dissociable neural prediction error signals underlying model-based and model-free reinforcement learning. *Neuron*, 2010.

I. Goodfellow, Y. Bengio, and A. Courville. *Deep Learning*. MIT Press, 2016. `http://www.deeplearningbook.org` Accessed on 3.3.2018.

A. Gosavi. Reinforcement learning: A tutorial survey and recent advances. *INFORMS J. on Computing*, 2009.

X. Guo, S. Singh, H. Lee, R. L. Lewis, and X. Wang. Deep learning for real-time atari game play using offline monte-carlo tree search planning. In *Advances in Neural Information Processing Systems 27*. Curran Associates, Inc., 2014.

A. Gupta, R. Mendonca, Y. Liu, P. Abbeel, and S. Levine. Meta-Reinforcement Learning of Structured Exploration Strategies. *ArXiv e-prints*, Feb. 2018.

N. Hansen and A. Ostermeier. Adapting arbitrary normal mutation distributions in evolution strategies: The covariance matrix adaptation. In *Evolutionary Computation, 1996., Proceedings of IEEE International Conference on*. IEEE, 1996.

M. Hessel, J. Modayil, H. van Hasselt, T. Schaul, G. Ostrovski, W. Dabney, D. Horgan, B. Piot, M. Azar, and D. Silver. Rainbow: Combining Improvements in Deep Reinforcement Learning. *ArXiv e-prints*, 2017.

J. H. Holland. Genetic algorithms. *Scientific American*, 1992.

R. Houthooft, X. Chen, Y. Duan, J. Schulman, F. De Turck, and P. Abbeel. Curiosity-driven exploration in deep reinforcement learning via bayesian neural networks. *ArXiv e-prints*, 2016.

S. Ioffe and C. Szegedy. Batch Normalization: Accelerating Deep Network Training by Reducing Internal Covariate Shift. *ArXiv e-prints*, Feb. 2015.

M. Johnson, K. Hofmann, T. Hutton, and D. Bignell. The malmo platform for artificial intelligence experimentation. In *Proceedings of the Twenty-Fifth International Joint Conference on Artificial Intelligence*, IJCAI'16. AAAI Press, 2016.

L. P. Kaelbling, M. L. Littman, and A. W. Moore. Reinforcement Learning: A Survey. *Journal of Artificial Intelligence Research*, 1996.

S. Kakade and J. Langford. Approximately Optimal Approximate Reinforcement Learning. *Proceedings of the 19th International Conference on Machine Learning*, 2002.

S. M. Kakade. A natural policy gradient. In *Advances in neural information processing systems*, 2002.

J. Kober, J. Peters, and J. A. Bagnell. Reinforcement Learning in Robotics: A Survey. In *Reinforcement Learning*. Springer, 2012.

A. Krizhevsky, I. Sutskever, and G. E. Hinton. Imagenet classification with deep convolutional neural networks. In *Advances in Neural Information Processing Systems 25*. Curran Associates, Inc., 2012.

Y. Lecun, Y. Bengio, and G. Hinton. Deep learning. *Nature*, 2015.

J. Lehman and K. O. Stanley. Abandoning objectives: Evolution through the search for novelty alone. *Evolutionary computation*, 2011.

Y. Li. Deep Reinforcement Learning: An Overview. *ArXiv e-prints*, Jan. 2017.

T. P. Lillicrap, J. J. Hunt, A. Pritzel, N. Heess, T. Erez, Y. Tassa, D. Silver, and D. Wierstra. Continuous Control with Deep Reinforcement Learning. *ArXiv e-prints*, 2015.

L.-j. Lin. *Reinforcement Learning for Robots Using Neural Networks*. PhD thesis, 1993.

V. Mnih, K. Kavukcuoglu, D. Silver, A. Graves, I. Antonoglou, D. Wierstra, and M. Riedmiller. Playing Atari with Deep Reinforcement Learning. *arXiv*, 2013.

V. Mnih, K. Kavukcuoglu, D. Silver, A. A. Rusu, J. Veness, M. G. Bellemare, A. Graves, M. Riedmiller, A. K. Fidjeland, G. Ostrovski, S. Petersen, C. Beattie, A. Sadik, I. Antonoglou, H. King, D. Kumaran, D. Wierstra, S. Legg, and D. Hassabis. Human-level control through deep reinforcement learning. *Nature*, 2015.

V. Mnih, A. Badia, M. Mirza, A. Graves, and T. Lillicrap. Asynchronous methods for deep reinforcement learning. *Icml*, 2016.

S. S. Mousavi, M. Schukat, and E. Howley. Deep reinforcement learning: an overview. In *Proceedings of SAI Intelligent Systems Conference*. Springer, 2016.

O. Nachum, M. Norouzi, and D. Schuurmans. Improving Policy Gradient by Exploring Under-appreciated Rewards. *ArXiv e-prints*, 2016.

A. Nagabandi, G. Kahn, R. S. Fearing, and S. Levine. Neural Network Dynamics for Model-Based Deep Reinforcement Learning with Model-Free Fine-Tuning. *ArXiv e-prints*, 2017.

A. Nair, P. Srinivasan, S. Blackwell, C. Alcicek, R. Fearon, A. De Maria, V. Panneershel-vam, M. Suleyman, C. Beattie, S. Petersen, S. Legg, V. Mnih, K. Kavukcuoglu, and D. Silver. Massively parallel methods for deep reinforcement learning. *ICML Deep Learning Workshop*, 2015.

A. Nair, B. McGrew, M. Andrychowicz, W. Zaremba, and P. Abbeel. Overcoming Exploration in Reinforcement Learning with Demonstrations. *ArXiv e-prints*, 2017.

A. Y. Ng, S. J. Russell, et al. Algorithms for inverse reinforcement learning. In *Icml*, 2000.

M. A. Nielsen. *Neural Networks and Deep Learning*. Determination Press, 2015. URL http://neuralnetworksanddeeplearning.com. Accessed on 3.3.2018.

J. Oh, V. Chockalingam, S. Singh, and H. Lee. Control of Memory, Active Perception, and Action in Minecraft. *ArXiv e-prints*, 2016.

OpenAI. Dota 2, n.d. URL https://blog.openai.com/dota-2/. Accessed 29.01.2018.

F. Petroski Such, V. Madhavan, E. Conti, J. Lehman, K. O. Stanley, and J. Clune. Deep Neuroevolution: Genetic Algorithms Are a Competitive Alternative for Training Deep Neural Networks for Reinforcement Learning. *ArXiv e-prints*, 2017.

I. Rechenberg and M. Eigen. Evolutionsstrategie-Optimierung technischer Systeme nach Prinzipien der biologischen Evolution. *Frommann-Holzboog Stuttgart*, 1973.

M. Rowland, M. G. Bellemare, W. Dabney, R. Munos, and Y. Whye Teh. An Analysis of Categorical Distributional Reinforcement Learning. *ArXiv e-prints*, 2018.

T. Salimans, I. Goodfellow, W. Zaremba, V. Cheung, A. Radford, and X. Chen. Improved techniques for training gans. In *Advances in Neural Information Processing Systems*, 2016.

T. Salimans, J. Ho, X. Chen, S. Sidor, and I. Sutskever. Evolution Strategies as a Scalable Alternative to Reinforcement Learning. *ArXiv e-prints*, 2017.

T. Schaul, J. Quan, I. Antonoglou, and D. Silver. Prioritized Experience Replay. *ArXiv e-prints*, 2015.

J. Schulman, S. Levine, P. Moritz, M. I. Jordan, and P. Abbeel. Trust Region Policy Optimization. *ArXiv e-prints*, 2015.

D. Silver. Reinforcement learning course, lecture 2: Markov decision process, 2015. URL http://www0.cs.ucl.ac.uk/staff/d.silver/web/Teaching_files/MDP.pdf. Accessed on 3.1.2018.

D. Silver. Tutorial: Deep Reinforcement Learning. In *A Conference Meeting at ICML*, 2016. URL https://icml.cc/Conferences/2016/tutorials/deep_rl_tutorial. pdf. Accessed on 3.1.2018.

D. Silver, G. Lever, N. Heess, T. Degris, D. Wierstra, and M. Riedmiller. Deterministic Policy Gradient Algorithms. *Proceedings of the 31st International Conference on Machine Learning (ICML-14)*, 2014.

D. Silver, A. Huang, C. J. Maddison, A. Guez, L. Sifre, G. van den Driessche, J. Schrittwieser, I. Antonoglou, V. Panneershelvam, M. Lanctot, S. Dieleman, D. Grewe,

J. Nham, N. Kalchbrenner, I. Sutskever, T. Lillicrap, M. Leach, K. Kavukcuoglu, T. Graepel, and D. Hassabis. Mastering the game of go with deep neural networks and tree search. *Nature*, 2016.

D. Silver, J. Schrittwieser, K. Simonyan, I. Antonoglou, A. Huang, A. Guez, T. Hubert, L. Baker, M. Lai, A. Bolton, Y. Chen, T. Lillicrap, F. Hui, L. Sifre, G. Van Den Driessche, T. Graepel, and D. Hassabis. Mastering the game of Go without human knowledge. *Nature*, 2017.

S. Smith. Learning to play stratego with convolutional neural networks. *Stanford University*, 2015.

R. Sutton and A. Barto. *Reinforcement Learning: An Introduction - Second Edition in Progress.* 2017.

R. S. Sutton. Learning to predict by the methods of temporal differences. *Mach. Learn.*, 1988.

I. Szita and A. Lörincz. Learning Tetris using the noisy cross-entropy method. *Neural computation*, 2006.

M. Tan. Multi-agent reinforcement learning: Independent vs. cooperative agents. In *Proceedings of the tenth international conference on machine learning*, 1993.

H. Tang, R. Houthooft, D. Foote, A. Stooke, O. X. Chen, Y. Duan, J. Schulman, F. De-Turck, and P. Abbeel. # Exploration: A Study of Count-Based Exploration for Deep Reinforcement Learning. In *Advances in Neural Information Processing Systems*, 2017.

C. Tessler, S. Givony, T. Zahavy, D. J. Mankowitz, and S. Mannor. A Deep Hierarchical Approach to Lifelong Learning in Minecraft. *ArXiv e-prints*, 2016.

E. L. Thorndike. The Law of Effect. *The American Journal of Psychology*, 1927.

S. Thrun and A. Schwartz. Issues in Using Function Approximation for Reinforcement Learning. *Proceedings of the 4th Connectionist Models Summer School Hillsdale, NJ. Lawrence Erlbaum*, 1993.

S. B. Thrun. Efficient Exploration In Reinforcement Learning. Technical report, 1992.

E. Todorov, T. Erez, and Y. Tassa. Mujoco: A physics engine for model-based control. In *Intelligent Robots and Systems (IROS), 2012 IEEE/RSJ International Conference on*. IEEE, 2012.

H. van Hasselt. Double q-learning. In *Advances in Neural Information Processing Systems 23*. Curran Associates, Inc., 2010.

H. van Hasselt, A. Guez, and D. Silver. Deep Reinforcement Learning with Double Q-learning. *ArXiv e-prints*, Sept. 2015.

Z. Wang, T. Schaul, M. Hessel, H. van Hasselt, M. Lanctot, and N. de Freitas. Dueling Network Architectures for Deep Reinforcement Learning. *ArXiv e-prints*, 2015.

C. J. Watkins and P. Dayan. Q-learning. *Machine learning*, 1992.

C. J. C. H. Watkins. *Learning from delayed rewards*. PhD thesis, King's College, Cambridge, 1989.

D. Wierstra, T. Schaul, J. Peters, and J. Schmidhuber. Natural evolution strategies. In *Evolutionary Computation, 2008. CEC 2008.(IEEE World Congress on Computational Intelligence). IEEE Congress on*. IEEE, 2008.

D. Wierstra, T. Schaul, T. Glasmachers, Y. Sun, J. Peters, and J. Schmidhuber. Natural evolution strategies. *Journal of Machine Learning Research*, 2014.

J. Wilich. Reinforcement learning for heroes of newerth, 2015. Bachelor Thesis.

A. Wilson, A. Fern, S. Ray, and P. Tadepalli. Learning and transferring roles in multiagent reinforcement. In *Proc. AAAI-08 Workshop on Transfer Learning for Complex Tasks*, 2008.

Y. Zhu, R. Mottaghi, E. Kolve, J. J. Lim, A. Gupta, L. Fei-Fei, and A. Farhadi. Target-driven Visual Navigation in Indoor Scenes using Deep Reinforcement Learning. *ArXiv e-prints*, 2016.